The Science of Getting Things Done

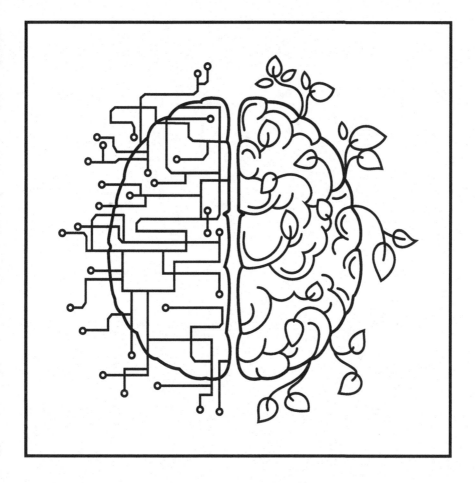

Jess Davis, MEd, Elem I-II

DOING.

The Science of Getting Things Done

A Planner for Mastering Your Tasks

Jess Davis, MEd Elem I-II

Montessori Minds

authorHOUSE®

AuthorHouse™
1663 Liberty Drive
Bloomington, IN 47403
www.authorhouse.com
Phone: 833-262-8899

Published by AuthorHouse   02/05/2025

ISBN: 979-8-8230-4206-2 (sc)
ISBN: 979-8-8230-4205-5 (e)

Library of Congress Control Number: 2025901122

Print information available on the last page.

This book is printed on acid-free paper.

THE BIG IDEAS

Welcome to **DOING**: *The Science of Getting Things Done*, a planner to teach, practice, and apply executive function skills for students approximately ages 9-15. This planner is most effective when used in conjunction with the DOING curriculum, available on MontessoriMindsConsulting.com.

Life is rich and complex and there are lots of important factors for deciding how we spend our days. Productivity (**DOING** things in an effective manner; getting things done on time) is not what your whole life should be focused on. Self-discovery, relaxation, creativity, bonds with friends and family...these are all just as important or more so. The more efficiently we complete required tasks, the more space we have for these pleasures of life.

It's an unavoidable truth that sometimes we just need to get things done. For school, for acquiring skills (like practicing an instrument), for contribution (such as helping with household chores)...It's also true that we will like some of these tasks more than others.

1. **When there are things we just need to get done, it's helpful to have the skills to be the master of the tasks instead of letting the tasks master you!** We've all had the experience of struggling to move forward with a task we dread, and it swallows our whole day.
2. It is essential to have a growth mindset. **Humans can achieve ANYTHING they set their minds to if they are strategic, set smart goals, and work hard toward those goals.**
3. The mental skills that help us get things done in an effective way are called Executive Function Skills. Research shows that **Executive Function Skills are learnable**-we can build our own abilities to get things done. **There is a science to productivity, and anyone can access it.**

A person who understands the science of **DOING** has a research-based skill toolbox to help them conquer tasks, which ensures they have time for all of those important, balanced priorities in their lives. Tasks have four parts, and often during our day this is a repeated cycle:

- Task Initiation (getting started)
- Concentration (staying focused and making continuous progress)
- Task Completion (being "done" and moving on)
- Transition (to your next activity)

This planner is designed to help you be an action researcher to design the conditions and practices that best allow you to be the master of your task cycle. This will help you achieve your productivity goals and will also help you create space for other passions in your life (like playing soccer with friends). Life is about balance-don't let your task list control you.

This planner gives you the structure to master one quarter (9 weeks). Introductions to evidence-based tools are found throughout the planner, helping you build the toolbox you need to master **the science of DOING.**

But WHY? do we need to get things done? How can it be proved to you that it's really important to do the work of completing tasks--even the ones you don't want to do?

Your brain has a way to help you with this. The fancy word for it is nonverbal working memory, but we are going to call it "if/then thinking". This strategy can be happening instantly sometimes, without us even being aware of it, and sometimes we may need to think through it on purpose. Our brain runs through what will happen if we make a decision (or don't make a decision). It's like an imaginary "practice run" for life. It helps us think about how our different actions will create different results in our lives, and how each of those results would make us feel. This helps us pick the best decision to make to get the most pleasant result for ourselves.

I'm going to use the example of brushing my teeth. It seems like such a simple task, but I actually have a lot of different choices available. I could:

1. Go upstairs quickly and brush my teeth well.
2. Skip brushing my teeth and lie about it if my mom asks.
3. Skip brushing my teeth and tell my mom, then have an argument.
4. Put off brushing my teeth, then do it when my mom asks as we are ready to leave.
5. Brush my teeth quickly, so I can say I did it (but not well).
6. Put it out of my mind and not think about it ever again.

How do I know which choice is best? My brain considers what will happen if I do each choice. Some would be good. Some would be bad. This helps me pick the right decision. For example:

Brushing Teeth	
IF	Then...
Brush well	My teeth will be healthy, no conflict with parent
Skip, lie	Teeth unhealthy, no conflict with parent
Skip, argue	Teeth unhealthy, conflict with parent
Brush late	Late to school, possible conflict with parent
Brush quickly	Perhaps unhealthy teeth, probably no conflict with parent
Forget	Unhealthy teeth, possible conflict with parent if they ask

SKILL BUILDER — If/Then Thinking

Now you try. Choose one task that you need to do and think of all your possible choices for how to handle it. Put each choice in the "if" column. Then think about what the result will be if you do that choice and put this in the "then" column.

Task:		
IF (I do this...)	Then...(this is likely to happen.)	I'd probably feel...

Rate Your Skills and Watch Your Growth

Each skill builder will have you rate yourself on the new skills and strategies that have been introduced. You don't need to be good at it yet! Keep practicing and you will see your progress. When this planner is full, go back through and revisit these questions to see if your answers have changed.

I can list many action choices. ☆ ☆ ☆ ☆ ☆

I can imagine the result of each action and how I would feel. ☆ ☆ ☆ ☆ ☆

🧠What are EF Skills?

Executive function (EF) skills are cognitive skills, or thinking skills, that help us plan, organize, prioritize, and do tasks. They also help us control our emotions and impulses and make good decisions. Executive function skills are essential for success in our school, work, and personal lives.

Executive function skills include planning, time management, metacognition (thinking about thinking), emotional self-regulation (self-control), memory, flexibility, impulse control, attention, organization, task initiation, perseverance, goal setting, self-awareness, self-monitoring, response inhibition (think before you act), prioritizing, problem-solving, sequencing, and more! This sounds like a lot, but once we build them as habits they don't feel like "work" anymore-they are processes we do automatically as we move through tasks, without even thinking about them.

Complete the **Executive Skills Inventory** on the next page. Think about whether each of the below EF skills are something you want to learn, something you are practicing, or something you are mastering.
- **Want to learn:** maybe you've heard of it, but it doesn't feel like a personal strength for you yet and right now you don't practice it regularly.
- **Practicing:** You know what it is and that you should do it, and you remember to practice sometimes. Sometimes you need reminders.
- **Mastering:** You know what it is, why it's important, and you have set an intention to make it a regular habit. You do it most of the time, and usually without reminders from others. It is going well for you and you feel pretty good at it.

You will do this exercise again at the end of the planner, and see how much you have grown. This challenge is asking you to practice several executive function skills:
- memory
- metacognition
- self-awareness
- self-monitoring

4

Executive Skills Inventory
Beginning of the Quarter

	Want to Learn	Learning	Mastering
Planning I can break down big projects into manageable steps and estimate how long each step will take me pretty accurately.	☐	☐	☐
Time Management I can get everything done before deadlines, and know how to strategize which tasks to do first to stay on top of everything.	☐	☐	☐
Concentration I can sustain focus for long periods of time, even on tasks I don't "like". My mind, hands, body, and eyes can be only on the task in front of me for 20-60 minutes at a time.	☐	☐	☐
Self-control I can notice urges to do things that don't align with my goals and values, and I can stop myself from doing them before they happen, even when this means doing something I don't like.	☐	☐	☐
Memory I can remember instructions, lists, and facts both in the short-term and for longer-term needs. When I need this information to help me complete a task or meet a goal, I can recall it easily and accurately.	☐	☐	☐
Flexibility I understand things don't always go as planned, and when the unexpected happens I can make in-the-moment decisions that I feel proud of now and later. Changes don't stress me out because I know they are a natural part of life.	☐	☐	☐
Attention I can choose what my brain pays attention to, even if it's something that doesn't feel "fun". My brain can filter out sounds, sights, and thoughts I don't need to help me focus.	☐	☐	☐
Organization I can organize my belongings and thoughts in ways that make sense to myself and others. I use organization as a tool to help me complete tasks more easily.	☐	☐	☐
Task Initiation I can see a project as a series of small tasks, and a task as a series of steps. I can start the first step independently and quickly, even when I don't feel like it.	☐	☐	☐
Perseverance I can "push through" a task I don't want to do. This can be when it feels boring, long, or hard. Even though I'd like to quit, I keep going.	☐	☐	☐

How to Use the Planner

Planners are an important tool that make executive function skills "visible" by providing a structure that encourages us to apply them. Studies show that having a written plan can increase productivity (*Getting Things Done, 2016*). The parts of the planner explained below will serve as cues to use the EF strategies you learn along the way in this planner. Also, scientists have come to understand that multi-tasking is a myth (*The Myth of Multitasking, 2014*) and it's better to focus on one thing at a time. But which thing to focus on? And how to stay focused? This planner will help you make those smart decisions in the process of getting things done that help you meet your goals in any area of life.

Skill builder pages introduce you to an **evidence-based strategy** (supported by research) for getting things done. They often include a **challenge** to help you practice the skill. The skills will build on each other. We best digest small chunks of information at a time (for example, this is why we memorize phone numbers in sets of 3-4 digits instead of a string of ten digits). Therefore, the lessons are usually spread out with only one or two per week.

 Week of Each week starts with a **reflection** on the previous week, includes an **overview** of important events or due dates, and then **sets an intention** for the week ahead. Finally, you will use the **priority matrix** to organize your task list. (See *Priority Matrix Skill Builder* for information about this tool.)

- **Self-reflection** helps us process mistakes, identify questions we have, and create meaning from our experiences. One study found that people who took 15 minutes to reflect on what they learned at the end of the day performed 23% better after 10 days compared to those who did not take time to reflect (*Learning by Thinking, 2014*). In another study, people who reflected during their commute showed increased happiness and productivity and decreased burnout (*Reflecting on Work Improves Job Performance, 2014*).
- Creating an **Overview** of your week is basically summarizing the most important notes for the next 7 days that you will need to consider. This is an important skill because it helps you condense a lot of information into manageable ideas and identify the key important notes of the week, allowing you to focus on the details later in your daily planning.
- Setting **Intentions** is about going beyond just checking a box for a finished task. Intentions align our actions with our core values and beliefs, acting as a compass for our week.

How to Use the Planner

Daily Planning and Doing

The daily planning pages provide a structure for applying various Executive Function strategies each day. This uses two Evidence-based Practices (EBPs):
- Using **graphic organizers** for mental organization of ideas
- **Making thinking visible,** combining ideas from two EBPs called "Mind Mapping" and Harvard's Project Zero, which help us visualize, organize and remember information.

Graphic Organizers are effective because they help us:
- Organize information visually
- Make connections
- Create a plan
- Communicate effectively
- Simplify complex information

Making Thinking Visible involves two practices from EBPs:
- Identifying hierarchical relationships: In the case of this planner, that's understanding that projects are made of tasks and tasks are made of steps. Our thinking when we plan, too, has to go from the "big picture" down to the details. Mind Mapping is an EBP that focuses on mapping hierarchical relationships.
- Building thinking routines (patterns and strategies for organizing and using information) specifically some related to using executive function skills to complete tasks. Thinking Routines is also a term used as part of the research done by Project Zero at Harvard University.

A Note About Building a "Strategy Toolbox"

We all likely have a toolbox at home. Just because it has a hammer in it doesn't mean we should use it! The key is picking the right tool for the task we are trying to complete. Our strategy toolboxes are the same way. Trying each strategy helps us know if we like it, when it might be most useful, etc. Then, when we face a challenge, we have many strategies to choose from to help us meet our goals. YOU are the expert on whether a strategy is helpful for you. Part of the experience of using this planner is learning more about *yourself*.

How to Use the Planner

 ## Daily Planning and Doing

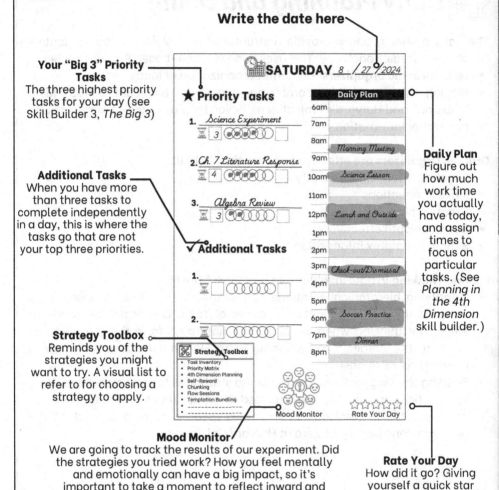

Write the date here

Your "Big 3" Priority Tasks
The three highest priority tasks for your day (see Skill Builder 3, *The Big 3*)

Additional Tasks
When you have more than three tasks to complete independently in a day, this is where the tasks go that are not your top three priorities.

Strategy Toolbox
Reminds you of the strategies you might want to try. A visual list to refer to for choosing a strategy to apply.

Daily Plan
Figure out how much work time you actually have today, and assign times to focus on particular tasks. (See *Planning in the 4th Dimension* skill builder.)

Mood Monitor
We are going to track the results of our experiment. Did the strategies you tried work? How you feel mentally and emotionally can have a big impact, so it's important to take a moment to reflect inward and make a note of how you felt today.

Rate Your Day
How did it go? Giving yourself a quick star rating is a mini-self-reflection for each day.

One Piece at a Time
You don't have to start using all the pieces right away. This planner will teach you one part at a time, starting with knowing how to Inventory Tasks (Skill Builder 1) and Prioritize Tasks (Skill Builder 2). Use the pieces you know, and build as you go. Try your best to use new strategies consistently for a while before you decide whether you like them or not. Building new habits requires multiple repetitions before they start feeling natural or easy, so you have to get through that challenge before you truly know whether the tool works for you. Try daily habits every day for at least two weeks and weekly habits for at least a month before you judge them.

Task Inventories, also known as the To-Do List, are the first step in organizing ourselves and getting ready to be productive. First, we need to know everything we should be doing, and when we are supposed to have it done. Use the space below to make a list of ALL the things you need to do this week. Keep thinking about it for a while, and add things as you think of them. Keep adding to it as new things come up.

Task	Due Date	Task	Due Date
○		○	
○		○	
○		○	
○		○	
○		○	
○		○	
○		○	
○		○	
○		○	
○		○	
○		○	
○		○	
○		○	
○		○	
○		○	
○		○	
○		○	
○		○	
○		○	
○		○	

Rate Your Skills and Watch Your Growth

Each skill builder will have you rate yourself on the new skills and strategies that have been introduced. You don't need to be good at it yet! Keep practicing and you will see your progress. When this planner is full, go back through and revisit these questions to see if your answers have changed.

I know what I need to get done. ☆ ☆ ☆ ☆ ☆

I know the date things need to be done. ☆ ☆ ☆ ☆ ☆

If there's not a due date, I can set my own reasonable time goal for getting a task done. ☆ ☆ ☆ ☆ ☆

S.T.O.P.
AND READ THE ROOM

Having a complete list of our tasks just checks our awareness of what we need to do. It does not actually help us get things done. We need to understand the **context** of a task. The context gives us more information, like "who, what, where, when, why", about the task. This helps us effectively prioritize, prepare, initiate, progress, and complete the task. Speech and Language Pathologists Sarah Ward and Kristen Jacobsen created the S.T.O.P. and read the room strategy for understanding more about the context of a task. It gives us a tool for remembering to think about *how* we will get things done, not just that we need to do them.

S=Space (Where do I need to be/go?)

T=Time (When do I need to do it/how long will it take?)

O= Objects (What things do I need to do it?)

P=People (Who do I need to work with? Who am I doing it "for?" What is *my* role/benefit?)

For example, if your task is to brush your teeth:
S (Space)-go into the bathroom
T (Time)-before leaving for school
O (Objects)-get toothbrush, paste, floss, and water
P (Person)-self-care for me so that my teeth are healthy; my parent will also be expecting me to have it done when I come downstairs and will be frustrated if I say no.

On the next page, use your task list to break down some of the things you need to do using the S.T.O.P. model. Is there a task that often causes conflict for you, such as frustration between you and a parent or teacher? If so, these might be good ones to practice with, and perhaps you could even go over it with the adult involved. Sometimes this is a great way to discover the root of a misunderstanding.

Challenge: Choose two tasks from the list you created and complete the S.T.O.P. charts below.

Task:			
S	Space	Where?	
T	Time	When? By?	
O	Objects	Need?	
P	Person	Why? Who?	

Task:			
S	Space	Where?	
T	Time	When? By?	
O	Objects	Need?	
P	Person	Why? Who?	

Rate Your Skills and Watch Your Growth

Each skill builder will have you rate yourself on the new skills and strategies that have been introduced. You don't need to be good at it yet! Keep practicing and you will see your progress. When this planner is full, go back through and revisit these questions to see if your answers have changed.

I can imagine the context of a task before it happens.

☆ ☆ ☆ ☆ ☆

I understand how the context of a task might change my actions to get it done.

☆ ☆ ☆ ☆ ☆

BUILDER PRIORITY MATRIX

A to-do list tells us *what* to do, but not *which task* to do first. The priority matrix is one tool to help us decide which tasks are our "priorities"-the most important things we should tackle first. Our priority matrix is adapted from one US President Dwight Eisenhower made famous (his version is often called the "Eisenhower Matrix").

- Things that need done really soon (they are "urgent") and are important (other people are counting on you, the project builds next week, you won't have access to things you need to complete the task if you don't get it done on time, etc.) are in the **URGENT** box and need to be addressed first.
- Things that are important, but don't necessarily need to be done right now, go in the **IMPORTANT** box.
- Things that aren't big, important items and don't need done RIGHT NOW, but that need done for us to meet our goals or obligations, go in the **NEED DONE** box.
- Things that would add value, but it would be ok if we don't get them done, go in the **WOULD BE NICE** box.

Knowing what questions to ask yourself to sort the tasks can be the hard part. If you're not sure, this is a great discussion to have with an adult to make a list specific to your situation. Typical questions include:

1. Is the task due very soon?
2. Does it feel very large? (I think I should get started because it will take a long time.)
3. Is there a group depending on me?
4. Will materials or resources I need become unavailable if I don't get it done on time?
5. Is there a "part 2" that will build on this task? If I fall behind, will it make me even more behind next week and cause me stress?

Challenge:

What other questions might help you decide if a task is URGENT?

_____

_____

_____

_____

BUILDER PRIORITY MATRIX
Practice

CHALLENGE: *Use the task inventory (to-do list) you made in the previous skill builder and sort your tasks into the priority matrix.*

Priority Matrix

URGENT	IMPORTANT
NEEDS DONE	**WOULD BE NICE**

Rate Your Skills and Watch Your Growth

I understand **why** I should do urgent tasks first. ☆ ☆ ☆ ☆ ☆

I know what questions to ask myself to decide how to sort tasks into the priority matrix. ☆ ☆ ☆ ☆ ☆

THE BIG 3

One EBP is "The Rule of Three" (*Getting Results the Agile Way*, 2010). It is a productivity system that helps narrow your focus. Instead of trying to do *everything*, you focus on your most important three items. By spreading your attention and energy to fewer tasks, you can increase focus and get better results. This can be especially helpful if you feel overwhelmed by the number of things you need to get done. (We will talk later about feeling overwhelmed by the *size* of projects.)

Challenge: Use the Priority Matrix you completed for the last Skill Builder to identify your "Big 3" tasks.

1. Start with the urgent tasks. If you have more than three urgent tasks, decide which is the MOST urgent, second-most urgent, and third-most urgent and record these on the lines below.
2. If you have less than three urgent tasks, record the urgent tasks first (in order of urgency or importance), then look at the "important" box. Decide which is MOST important, and this would be your next priority after your urgent tasks.
3. If you only have one item in urgent and one in important, then the most important "needs done" task would come next.

MY BIG 3

1._____

2._____

3._____

Even when I have a long list of things to do, I can name the three highest-priority tasks. ☆ ☆ ☆ ☆ ☆

I can stay focused on my Big 3 tasks until they are done. ☆ ☆ ☆ ☆ ☆

📅 Week of ___ / ___ / ___

Reflect on the Past Week

_____

_____

_____

📅 Weekly Overview 📅

Monday

Tuesday

Wednesday

Thursday

Friday

Saturday

Sunday

Set an Intention for the Week Ahead

_____

_____

_____

Priority Matrix

URGENT	IMPORTANT

NEEDS DONE	WOULD BE NICE

Habit Tracker

	☐☐☐☐☐☐☐☐☐☐☐☐☐☐
_____	☐☐☐☐☐☐☐☐☐☐☐☐☐☐
_____	☐☐☐☐☐☐☐☐☐☐☐☐☐☐
_____	☐☐☐☐☐☐☐☐☐☐☐☐☐☐
_____	☐☐☐☐☐☐☐☐☐☐☐☐☐☐

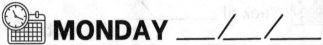 **MONDAY** ___/___/___

★ Priority Tasks

Daily Plan

1. _____

🕰 ☐ ⓞⓞⓞⓞⓞ ☐

2. _____

🕰 ☐ ⓞⓞⓞⓞⓞ ☐

3. _____

🕰 ☐ ⓞⓞⓞⓞⓞ ☐

✓ Additional Tasks

1. _____

🕰 ☐ ⓞⓞⓞⓞⓞ ☐

2. _____

🕰 ☐ ⓞⓞⓞⓞⓞ ☐

Daily Plan

- 6am
- 7am
- 8am
- 9am
- 10am
- 11am
- 12pm
- 1pm
- 2pm
- 3pm
- 4pm
- 5pm
- 6pm
- 7pm
- 8pm

 Strategy Toolbox

- Task Inventory
- Priority Matrix
- 4th Dimension Planning
- Self-Reward
- Chunking
- Flow Sessions
- Temptation Bundling
- _____
- _____

Mood Monitor

Rate Your Day

 **TUESDAY** ___/___/___

★ Priority Tasks

1. _____

⏳ ☐ ◯◯◯◯◯ ☐

2. _____

⏳ ☐ ◯◯◯◯◯ ☐

3. _____

⏳ ☐ ◯◯◯◯◯ ☐

✓ Additional Tasks

1. _____

⏳ ☐ ◯◯◯◯◯ ☐

2. _____

⏳ ☐ ◯◯◯◯◯ ☐

Daily Plan
6am
7am
8am
9am
10am
11am
12pm
1pm
2pm
3pm
4pm
5pm
6pm
7pm
8pm

 Strategy Toolbox

- Task Inventory
- Priority Matrix
- 4th Dimension Planning
- Self-Reward
- Chunking
- Flow Sessions
- Temptation Bundling
- _____
- _____

Mood Monitor

Rate Your Day

20

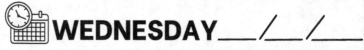

WEDNESDAY ___/___/___

★ Priority Tasks

1. _____

⏳ ☐ ⃝⃝⃝⃝⃝ ☐

2. _____

⏳ ☐ ⃝⃝⃝⃝⃝ ☐

3. _____

⏳ ☐ ⃝⃝⃝⃝⃝ ☐

✓ Additional Tasks

1. _____

⏳ ☐ ⃝⃝⃝⃝⃝ ☐

2. _____

⏳ ☐ ⃝⃝⃝⃝⃝ ☐

Daily Plan

Time	
6am	
7am	
8am	
9am	
10am	
11am	
12pm	
1pm	
2pm	
3pm	
4pm	
5pm	
6pm	
7pm	
8pm	

⚒ Strategy Toolbox

- Task Inventory
- Priority Matrix
- 4th Dimension Planning
- Self-Reward
- Chunking
- Flow Sessions
- Temptation Bundling
- _____
- _____

Mood Monitor

Rate Your Day ☆☆☆☆☆

🕐📅 THURSDAY ___/___/___

★ Priority Tasks

1. _____

⧖ ☐ ⬭⬭⬭⬭⬭ ☐

2. _____

⧖ ☐ ⬭⬭⬭⬭⬭ ☐

3. _____

⧖ ☐ ⬭⬭⬭⬭⬭ ☐

✓ Additional Tasks

1. _____

⧖ ☐ ⬭⬭⬭⬭⬭ ☐

2. _____

⧖ ☐ ⬭⬭⬭⬭⬭ ☐

🛠 Strategy Toolbox

- Task Inventory
- Priority Matrix
- 4th Dimension Planning
- Self-Reward
- Chunking
- Flow Sessions
- Temptation Bundling
- _____
- _____

Daily Plan
6am
7am
8am
9am
10am
11am
12pm
1pm
2pm
3pm
4pm
5pm
6pm
7pm
8pm

Mood Monitor

Rate Your Day

 **FRIDAY** ___/___/___

★ Priority Tasks

1. _____
   ⧗ [ ] ◯◯◯◯◯ [ ]

2. _____
   ⧗ [ ] ◯◯◯◯◯ [ ]

3. _____
   ⧗ [ ] ◯◯◯◯◯ [ ]

✓ Additional Tasks

1. _____
   ⧗ [ ] ◯◯◯◯◯ [ ]

2. _____
   ⧗ [ ] ◯◯◯◯◯ [ ]

🛠 Strategy Toolbox

- Task Inventory
- Priority Matrix
- 4th Dimension Planning
- Self-Reward
- Chunking
- Flow Sessions
- Temptation Bundling
- _____
- _____

Daily Plan
6am
7am
8am
9am
10am
11am
12pm
1pm
2pm
3pm
4pm
5pm
6pm
7pm
8pm

Mood Monitor

Rate Your Day

26

 **SATURDAY** ___/___/___

★ Priority Tasks

1. _____
⧗ ☐ ◯◯◯◯◯ ☐

2. _____
⧗ ☐ ◯◯◯◯◯ ☐

3. _____
⧗ ☐ ◯◯◯◯◯ ☐

✓ Additional Tasks

1. _____
⧗ ☐ ◯◯◯◯◯ ☐

2. _____
⧗ ☐ ◯◯◯◯◯ ☐

🛠 Strategy Toolbox

- Task Inventory
- Priority Matrix
- 4th Dimension Planning
- Self-Reward
- Chunking
- Flow Sessions
- Temptation Bundling
- _____
- _____

Daily Plan
6am
7am
8am
9am
10am
11am
12pm
1pm
2pm
3pm
4pm
5pm
6pm
7pm
8pm

Mood Monitor

Rate Your Day

SUNDAY ___ / ___ / ___

★ Priority Tasks

1. _____

⧗ ☐ ○○○○○ ☐

2. _____

⧗ ☐ ○○○○○ ☐

3. _____

⧗ ☐ ○○○○○ ☐

✓ Additional Tasks

1. _____

⧗ ☐ ○○○○○ ☐

2. _____

⧗ ☐ ○○○○○ ☐

Strategy Toolbox

- Task Inventory
- Priority Matrix
- 4th Dimension Planning
- Self-Reward
- Chunking
- Flow Sessions
- Temptation Bundling
- _____
- _____

Daily Plan
6am
7am
8am
9am
10am
11am
12pm
1pm
2pm
3pm
4pm
5pm
6pm
7pm
8pm

Mood Monitor

Rate Your Day

Having a lits of what needs done, and even understanding what needs done first, can still not be enough to ensure success. To understand whether we are setting reasonable goals for ourselves today, we have to start planning in "the fourth dimension". We've all heard of three dimensions (3D, like 3D printing), but what is the 4th dimension? **Time.**

Einstein's famous theory of relativity says that time is linked with space. Physicists define time as the progression of events from the past to the present to the future, making it a dimension used to describe events in three-dimensional space.

Now I have to admit, I don't really understand all of that, but my takeaway is that tasks really do take up "space" in our day, we need to think about this in terms of blocking off time in our schedule. There is only so much "space" in our day. For example, let's say I have fallen behind at work or school, and to be "caught up" I would need to get 18 tasks done today. Just putting 18 tasks on my list is not realistic–I only have a limited amount of time to get things done today between my driving time, meetings, lunch, etc. I have to first figure out how much time I actually have to devote to these tasks, then decide how many/which of the items will actually fit into my day (prioritizing the urgent/important tasks). I can make good progress toward getting "caught up," but I likely won't complete all 18 items.

One of the hardest parts about planning in 4D is "feeling" the passage of time and being able to estimate accurately how long something will take you. This is like asking you to predict the future! The best way to build this skill is to begin guessing how long things will take you, then actually timing them to see how close you were.

Challenge: Estimate and time the following activities to see how accurate your hypothesis is for how long each item will take.

Activity	Estimate	Result
brushing teeth		
eating dinner		
cleaning your room		

SKILL BUILDER
PLANNING IN THE Fourth dimension

The steps to planning in the 4th Dimension are:

1. Figure out how much time you have by **marking off** the time that is already taken. For example, during lessons or lunch or soccer practice, I will not be able to work on my projects. *In the example to the right, I have shaded and labeled the obligations I have during which I am unavailable for completing my task list.*

Challenge: On the next page, you will think about what time is usually "taken" during your week and not available for doing projects. Block out things like meals, practices, lessons, driving time, etc. to see what "space is left" in your standard week for planning your productivity.

2. Calculate how much time that leaves available. What "space is left" between your activities and obligations today? *In my example to the right, I only have about four and a half hours to do my own tasks today.*

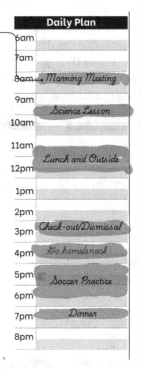

Daily Plan
6am
7am
8am — Morning Meeting
9am
Science Lesson
10am
11am
Lunch and Outside
12pm
1pm
2pm
3pm — Check-out/Dismissal
4pm — Go home/snack
5pm — Soccer Practice
6pm
7pm — Dinner
8pm

3. Look at your list of goals for today, and **estimate** how long each one will take you. In the first square box under each item, write how many minutes you think the task will take. After you complete the task, **record the result** in the second square box. Compare your hypothesis to your result. *In my example, I thought the algebra page would take me 40 minutes to complete, but it actually took me 55.*

3. Algebra Page
⏳ 40 ⦵⦵⦵⦵⦵ 55

- Did the task take you longer than expected?
  - If so, was this because your estimate was not very accurate, or because you struggled to focus during the task?
    - If your estimate was off, use this to inform and improve future estimation.
    - If you struggled to focus, look at your strategy toolbox and make a plan for what you could do to try to help yourself stay on track next time.

PLANNING IN THE *fourth dimension*

The Week At-A-Glance

Over the course of the week, what times do you usually know you will be unavailable to do your tasks? (Meals, driving, classes, practices, wind-downs before bed that your know you need, a standing date with friends you want to be sure to make space for, etc.) Shade in and label the times you are not available to be productive, then calculate how much "productive" time is usually left each day.

Mon

Daily Plan

6am
7am
8am
9am
10am
11am
12pm
1pm
2pm
3pm
4pm
5pm
6pm
7pm
8pm

Tue

Daily Plan

6am
7am
8am
9am
10am
11am
12pm
1pm
2pm
3pm
4pm
5pm
6pm
7pm
8pm

Wed

Daily Plan

6am
7am
8am
9am
10am
11am
12pm
1pm
2pm
3pm
4pm
5pm
6pm
7pm
8pm

Thu

Daily Plan

6am
7am
8am
9am
10am
11am
12pm
1pm
2pm
3pm
4pm
5pm
6pm
7pm
8pm

Fri

Daily Plan

6am
7am
8am
9am
10am
11am
12pm
1pm
2pm
3pm
4pm
5pm
6pm
7pm
8pm

Sat

Daily Plan

6am
7am
8am
9am
10am
11am
12pm
1pm
2pm
3pm
4pm
5pm
6pm
7pm
8pm

Sun

Daily Plan

6am
7am
8am
9am
10am
11am
12pm
1pm
2pm
3pm
4pm
5pm
6pm
7pm
8pm

Day	Time Available
Monday	
Tuesday	
Wednesday	
Thursday	
Friday	
Saturday	
Sunday	

Rate Your Skills and Watch Your Growth

I know how much work time I have available each day. ☆ ☆ ☆ ☆ ☆

I can estimate how long tasks will take me pretty accurately. ☆ ☆ ☆ ☆ ☆

34

Week of ___/___/___

Reflect on the Past Week

Weekly Overview

Monday	Tuesday	Wednesday

Thursday	Friday	Saturday
		Sunday

Set an Intention for the Week Ahead

Priority Matrix

URGENT	IMPORTANT

NEEDS DONE	WOULD BE NICE

Habit Tracker

	□ □ □ □ □ □ □ □ □ □ □ □ □
_____	□ □ □ □ □ □ □ □ □ □ □ □ □
_____	□ □ □ □ □ □ □ □ □ □ □ □ □
_____	□ □ □ □ □ □ □ □ □ □ □ □ □

 # MONDAY ___/___/___

★ Priority Tasks

1. _____
   ⏳ ☐ ⬭⬭⬭⬭⬭ ☐

2. _____
   ⏳ ☐ ⬭⬭⬭⬭⬭ ☐

3. _____
   ⏳ ☐ ⬭⬭⬭⬭⬭ ☐

✓ Additional Tasks

1. _____
   ⏳ ☐ ⬭⬭⬭⬭⬭ ☐

2. _____
   ⏳ ☐ ⬭⬭⬭⬭⬭ ☐

Daily Plan

| 6am |
| 7am |
| 8am |
| 9am |
| 10am |
| 11am |
| 12pm |
| 1pm |
| 2pm |
| 3pm |
| 4pm |
| 5pm |
| 6pm |
| 7pm |
| 8pm |

 ### Strategy Toolbox

- Task Inventory
- Priority Matrix
- 4th Dimension Planning
- Self-Reward
- Chunking
- Flow Sessions
- Temptation Bundling
- _____
- _____

Mood Monitor

Rate Your Day

 **TUESDAY** ___/___/___

★ Priority Tasks

1. _____

⏳ ☐ ⚪⚪⚪⚪⚪ ☐

2. _____

⏳ ☐ ⚪⚪⚪⚪⚪ ☐

3. _____

⏳ ☐ ⚪⚪⚪⚪⚪ ☐

✓ Additional Tasks

1. _____

⏳ ☐ ⚪⚪⚪⚪⚪ ☐

2. _____

⏳ ☐ ⚪⚪⚪⚪⚪ ☐

Daily Plan
6am
7am
8am
9am
10am
11am
12pm
1pm
2pm
3pm
4pm
5pm
6pm
7pm
8pm

🛠 Strategy Toolbox

- Task Inventory
- Priority Matrix
- 4th Dimension Planning
- Self-Reward
- Chunking
- Flow Sessions
- Temptation Bundling
- _____
- _____

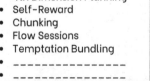

Mood Monitor

Rate Your Day

 **WEDNESDAY** ___/___/___

★ Priority Tasks

1. _____

⏳ ☐ ⦿⦿⦿⦿⦿ ☐

2. _____

⏳ ☐ ⦿⦿⦿⦿⦿ ☐

3. _____

⏳ ☐ ⦿⦿⦿⦿⦿ ☐

✓ Additional Tasks

1. _____

⏳ ☐ ⦿⦿⦿⦿⦿ ☐

2. _____

⏳ ☐ ⦿⦿⦿⦿⦿ ☐

Daily Plan
6am
7am
8am
9am
10am
11am
12pm
1pm
2pm
3pm
4pm
5pm
6pm
7pm
8pm

 Strategy Toolbox

- Task Inventory
- Priority Matrix
- 4th Dimension Planning
- Self-Reward
- Chunking
- Flow Sessions
- Temptation Bundling
- _____
- _____

Mood Monitor

Rate Your Day

THURSDAY ___/___/___

★ Priority Tasks

1. _____
   ⧗ □ ⟨⟨⟨⟨⟨⟩⟩⟩⟩⟩ □

2. _____
   ⧗ □ ⟨⟨⟨⟨⟨⟩⟩⟩⟩⟩ □

3. _____
   ⧗ □ ⟨⟨⟨⟨⟨⟩⟩⟩⟩⟩ □

✓ Additional Tasks

1. _____
   ⧗ □ ⟨⟨⟨⟨⟨⟩⟩⟩⟩⟩ □

2. _____
   ⧗ □ ⟨⟨⟨⟨⟨⟩⟩⟩⟩⟩ □

⚒ Strategy Toolbox

- Task Inventory
- Priority Matrix
- 4th Dimension Planning
- Self-Reward
- Chunking
- Flow Sessions
- Temptation Bundling
- _____
- _____

Daily Plan

6am	
7am	
8am	
9am	
10am	
11am	
12pm	
1pm	
2pm	
3pm	
4pm	
5pm	
6pm	
7pm	
8pm	

Mood Monitor

Rate Your Day

 **FRIDAY** ___/___/___

★ Priority Tasks

1. _____

⏳ ☐ ⃝⃝⃝⃝⃝ ☐

2. _____

⏳ ☐ ⃝⃝⃝⃝⃝ ☐

3. _____

⏳ ☐ ⃝⃝⃝⃝⃝ ☐

✓ Additional Tasks

1. _____

⏳ ☐ ⃝⃝⃝⃝⃝ ☐

2. _____

⏳ ☐ ⃝⃝⃝⃝⃝ ☐

Daily Plan
6am
7am
8am
9am
10am
11am
12pm
1pm
2pm
3pm
4pm
5pm
6pm
7pm
8pm

🛠 Strategy Toolbox

- Task Inventory
- Priority Matrix
- 4th Dimension Planning
- Self-Reward
- Chunking
- Flow Sessions
- Temptation Bundling
- _____
- _____

Mood Monitor

Rate Your Day

⏰📅 SATURDAY __/__/__

★ Priority Tasks

1. _____

⏳ ☐ ◯◯◯◯◯ ☐

2. _____

⏳ ☐ ◯◯◯◯◯ ☐

3. _____

⏳ ☐ ◯◯◯◯◯ ☐

✓ Additional Tasks

1. _____

⏳ ☐ ◯◯◯◯◯ ☐

2. _____

⏳ ☐ ◯◯◯◯◯ ☐

🛠 Strategy Toolbox

- Task Inventory
- Priority Matrix
- 4th Dimension Planning
- Self-Reward
- Chunking
- Flow Sessions
- Temptation Bundling
- _____
- _____

Daily Plan
6am
7am
8am
9am
10am
11am
12pm
1pm
2pm
3pm
4pm
5pm
6pm
7pm
8pm

Mood Monitor

Rate Your Day

 **SUNDAY** ___ / ___ / ___

★ Priority Tasks

1. _____

⏳ ☐ ⬭⬭⬭⬭⬭ ☐

2. _____

⏳ ☐ ⬭⬭⬭⬭⬭ ☐

3. _____

⏳ ☐ ⬭⬭⬭⬭⬭ ☐

✓ Additional Tasks

1. _____

⏳ ☐ ⬭⬭⬭⬭⬭ ☐

2. _____

⏳ ☐ ⬭⬭⬭⬭⬭ ☐

Daily Plan
6am
7am
8am
9am
10am
11am
12pm
1pm
2pm
3pm
4pm
5pm
6pm
7pm
8pm

 **Strategy Toolbox**

- Task Inventory
- Priority Matrix
- 4th Dimension Planning
- Self-Reward
- Chunking
- Flow Sessions
- Temptation Bundling
- _____
- _____

Mood Monitor

Rate Your Day

SKILL

Projects
Vs. Tasks

What is the difference between a project and a task?

Tasks are one thing we need to do. **Projects** are a series of tasks that build together to reach one goal over a longer period of time, needing more steps.

Projects can feel more intimidating. They can feel long or hard, and so we might avoid starting them. Often they are the thing on our plan that might not get finished. The first step is being self-aware enough to recognize which items you have these feelings about on your list.

We don't have to feel this way about projects! We can control how big they feel by how we organize the work. We learn to "unpack" larger projects and see the smaller tasks they are made of. Then we can break those tasks down into steps. Now the project doesn't feel so intimidating. We master our projects instead of letting them master us.

Steps to Unpacking a Project:
1. Notice the items on your to-do list that feel "hard" or "big". Is this because they are really a larger project with multiple layers?
2. Create a list of all the tasks required to complete the project. Each of these is one task for your task inventory. (See the next page for an example of breaking down a research paper.)
3. For each task, think about the steps involved and estimate how long it will take you.
4. Instead of putting the project on your daily plan, use the weekly planning page (or multiple weekly planners if it's a really long project) to map out how many tasks you will need to get done each day to get your project done by its deadline. Each of these tasks is now "due" on the day you have mapped it, and should be considered on your priority matrix.
5. If you stay on top of your tasks, before you know it your large project will be complete. However, it doesn't feel so "large" because you are only thinking about one smaller task at a time.

Projects
Vs. Tasks

Example: UNPACKING A PROJECT

PROJECT: WRITE A 5-PARAGRAPH RESEARCH ABOUT SLOTHS

TASKS

☐ *Subtopics*
Choose subtopics. Perhaps your rubric will help; I'm going to choose "what sloths eat", "where sloths live", and "how sloths move" as my subtopics. (10 minutes)

☐ *Resources*
Read through available resources and choose 3-4 based on headings, tables of contents, and indexes (looking for my subtopics). Learn about sloths, enjoy the books, and think about what is most important as you read. (30 minutes-depending on the sources, for example if they are books vs. articles, even this might need broken down into more steps).

☐ *Facts for Subtopic 1*
DEPENDING ON HOW YOUR BRAIN WORKS BEST...Maybe you read through all your resources, specifically looking for one subtopic, and take notes on at least 5 facts about what sloths eat, for example. Or maybe you focus on one resource and get facts about all three subtopics in your notes. I am going to organize my fact search by topic, so first I will collect at least 5 facts about what sloths eat. (30 minutes)

☐ *Facts for Subtopic 2*
Repeat with subtopic 2, where sloths live, collecting facts in your notes. (30 minutes)

☐ *Facts for Subtopic 3*
Repeat with subtopic 3, how sloths move, collecting facts in your notes. (30 minutes)

☐ *Write Body Paragraph 1*
Using your notes, write your first body paragraph about what sloths eat. (20 minutes)

Projects
Vs. Tasks

☐ *Write Body Paragraph 2*
Using your notes, write your second body paragraph (where sloths live). (20 minutes)

☐ *Write Body Paragraph 3*
Using your notes, write your third body paragraph (how sloths move). (20 minutes)

☐ *Intro Paragraph*
Using your three body paragraphs as a guide, write an introductory paragraph for your essay. (30 minutes)

☐ *Conclusion Paragraph*
Write a conclusion paragraph for your essay. (30 minutes)

☐ *Corrections*
After turning in your essay, address feedback as needed and turn in again (if applicable). (30 minutes)

Using the "UNPACKING" technique, this project that perhaps felt very large is now 12 tasks, each no bigger than reading or writing a paragraph. Each step is estimated to take 30 minutes or less.

There is no one "correct" way to break a project down into small tasks. Everyone's brain works differently. There are processes that are more effective or less effective, but even this can differ from person to person. Graphic organizers can be helpful, but each type of project often lends itself to a different graphic organizer. Find what works best for you!

If the NUMBER of tasks now feels overwhelming, one strategy is to literally make the rest invisible to yourself, and to focus on only one step at a time. For example, let's say you are feeling overwhelmed by algebra problems that take you 10-15 minutes each to complete. Perhaps there are twenty on the page, and this feels like A LOT. Copy the page, cut it into individual problems, and ask a friend, teacher, or parent to hand you one at a time. Remind yourself that, for now, that one algebra problem is all you have to do (because it is-you can handle the next one when it comes).

I can tell the difference between a project and a task. ☆ ☆ ☆ ☆ ☆

I can "unpack" a project into a list of short tasks. ☆ ☆ ☆ ☆ ☆

📅 Week of ___/___/___

Reflect on the Past Week

_____

_____

_____

📅 Weekly Overview 📅

Monday	Tuesday	Wednesday

Thursday	Friday	Saturday
		Sunday

Set an Intention for the Week Ahead

_____

_____

_____

Priority Matrix

URGENT	IMPORTANT

NEEDS DONE	WOULD BE NICE

_____

_____

_____

_____

Habit Tracker

_____ ☐☐☐☐☐☐☐☐☐☐☐☐☐☐

_____ ☐☐☐☐☐☐☐☐☐☐☐☐☐☐

_____ ☐☐☐☐☐☐☐☐☐☐☐☐☐☐

_____ ☐☐☐☐☐☐☐☐☐☐☐☐☐☐

 **MONDAY** ___/___/___

★ Priority Tasks

1._____
⏳ ☐ ⓞⓞⓞⓞⓞ ☐

2._____
⏳ ☐ ⓞⓞⓞⓞⓞ ☐

3._____
⏳ ☐ ⓞⓞⓞⓞⓞ ☐

✓ Additional Tasks

1._____
⏳ ☐ ⓞⓞⓞⓞⓞ ☐

2._____
⏳ ☐ ⓞⓞⓞⓞⓞ ☐

🛠 Strategy Toolbox

- Task Inventory
- Priority Matrix
- 4th Dimension Planning
- Self-Reward
- Chunking
- Flow Sessions
- Temptation Bundling
- _____
- _____

Daily Plan
6am
7am
8am
9am
10am
11am
12pm
1pm
2pm
3pm
4pm
5pm
6pm
7pm
8pm

Mood Monitor

Rate Your Day

 **TUESDAY** ___ / ___ / ___

★ Priority Tasks

1. _____

⏳ ☐ ⬡⬡⬡⬡⬡ ☐

2. _____

⏳ ☐ ⬡⬡⬡⬡⬡ ☐

3. _____

⏳ ☐ ⬡⬡⬡⬡⬡ ☐

✓ Additional Tasks

1. _____

⏳ ☐ ⬡⬡⬡⬡⬡ ☐

2. _____

⏳ ☐ ⬡⬡⬡⬡⬡ ☐

Daily Plan

6am	
7am	
8am	
9am	
10am	
11am	
12pm	
1pm	
2pm	
3pm	
4pm	
5pm	
6pm	
7pm	
8pm	

🛠 Strategy Toolbox

- Task Inventory
- Priority Matrix
- 4th Dimension Planning
- Self-Reward
- Chunking
- Flow Sessions
- Temptation Bundling
- _____
- _____

Mood Monitor

Rate Your Day ☆☆☆☆☆

WEDNESDAY___/___/___

★ Priority Tasks

1. _____

⌛ ☐ ◯◯◯◯◯ ☐

2. _____

⌛ ☐ ◯◯◯◯◯ ☐

3. _____

⌛ ☐ ◯◯◯◯◯ ☐

✓ Additional Tasks

1. _____

⌛ ☐ ◯◯◯◯◯ ☐

2. _____

⌛ ☐ ◯◯◯◯◯ ☐

🛠 Strategy Toolbox

- Task Inventory
- Priority Matrix
- 4th Dimension Planning
- Self-Reward
- Chunking
- Flow Sessions
- Temptation Bundling
- _____
- _____

Daily Plan
6am
7am
8am
9am
10am
11am
12pm
1pm
2pm
3pm
4pm
5pm
6pm
7pm
8pm

Mood Monitor

Rate Your Day

🕐📅 THURSDAY __/__/__

★ Priority Tasks

1. _____
⏳ ☐ ⬭⬭⬭⬭⬭ ☐

2. _____
⏳ ☐ ⬭⬭⬭⬭⬭ ☐

3. _____
⏳ ☐ ⬭⬭⬭⬭⬭ ☐

✓ Additional Tasks

1. _____
⏳ ☐ ⬭⬭⬭⬭⬭ ☐

2. _____
⏳ ☐ ⬭⬭⬭⬭⬭ ☐

🛠 Strategy Toolbox
- Task Inventory
- Priority Matrix
- 4th Dimension Planning
- Self-Reward
- Chunking
- Flow Sessions
- Temptation Bundling
- _____
- _____

Daily Plan
- 6am
- 7am
- 8am
- 9am
- 10am
- 11am
- 12pm
- 1pm
- 2pm
- 3pm
- 4pm
- 5pm
- 6pm
- 7pm
- 8pm

Mood Monitor

Rate Your Day

64

 **FRIDAY** ___/___/___

★ Priority Tasks

1. _____
⧗ [ ] ○○○○○ [ ]

2. _____
⧗ [ ] ○○○○○ [ ]

3. _____
⧗ [ ] ○○○○○ [ ]

✓ Additional Tasks

1. _____
⧗ [ ] ○○○○○ [ ]

2. _____
⧗ [ ] ○○○○○ [ ]

 **Strategy Toolbox**

- Task Inventory
- Priority Matrix
- 4th Dimension Planning
- Self-Reward
- Chunking
- Flow Sessions
- Temptation Bundling
- _____
- _____

Daily Plan
6am
7am
8am
9am
10am
11am
12pm
1pm
2pm
3pm
4pm
5pm
6pm
7pm
8pm

Mood Monitor

Rate Your Day

🕐📅 SATURDAY ___/___/___

★ Priority Tasks

1. _____
   ⏳ ☐ ◯◯◯◯◯ ☐

2. _____
   ⏳ ☐ ◯◯◯◯◯ ☐

3. _____
   ⏳ ☐ ◯◯◯◯◯ ☐

✓ Additional Tasks

1. _____
   ⏳ ☐ ◯◯◯◯◯ ☐

2. _____
   ⏳ ☐ ◯◯◯◯◯ ☐

🛠️ Strategy Toolbox

- Task Inventory
- Priority Matrix
- 4th Dimension Planning
- Self-Reward
- Chunking
- Flow Sessions
- Temptation Bundling
- _____
- _____

Daily Plan

| 6am |
| 7am |
| 8am |
| 9am |
| 10am |
| 11am |
| 12pm |
| 1pm |
| 2pm |
| 3pm |
| 4pm |
| 5pm |
| 6pm |
| 7pm |
| 8pm |

Mood Monitor

Rate Your Day

 **SUNDAY**___/___/___

★ Priority Tasks

1._____
⌛ ☐ ⬭⬭⬭⬭⬭ ☐

2._____
⌛ ☐ ⬭⬭⬭⬭⬭ ☐

3._____
⌛ ☐ ⬭⬭⬭⬭⬭ ☐

✓ Additional Tasks

1._____
⌛ ☐ ⬭⬭⬭⬭⬭ ☐

2._____
⌛ ☐ ⬭⬭⬭⬭⬭ ☐

Daily Plan
6am
7am
8am
9am
10am
11am
12pm
1pm
2pm
3pm
4pm
5pm
6pm
7pm
8pm

🛠 Strategy Toolbox

- Task Inventory
- Priority Matrix
- 4th Dimension Planning
- Self-Reward
- Chunking
- Flow Sessions
- Temptation Bundling
- _____
- _____

Mood Monitor

Rate Your Day

70

A distraction is something that takes your attention away from something you want to focus on. They can be internal or external.

Internal distractions:

- tiredness
- hunger
- illness
- worry
- daydreams

External Distractions:

- social interactions
- sounds
- sights
- physical feelings (like restless movements)

Ideally, our brain will prioritize what to focus on and will be able to block out distractions. Some people are able to filter out distractions more easily than others. People with attention disabilities have a particularly difficult time tuning out everything but what they want to focus on.

If you are struggling with distractions, here are some strategies to try:

- **Physically block the distraction**
  - Noise-canceling earbuds with nothing playing, for example, can block out distracting sounds
  - Working at a table facing a wall or in a corner or nook can help block visual distractions such as noticing what other people in the room are doing
- **Listen to your body**
  - If your body needs to move and you notice yourself fidgeting or rocking from the discomfort, the best thing is to find a moment to get some movement. You could continue to try to focus, fighting the urge to move, or you could go run around the block or do some stretching in a corner to help you settle into some better focus time in a few minutes.
  - If you find you focus better when moving your body a little, there are tools for this. There are seat cushions that let you bounce or rock, or fidget items for your hands.
- **Push through, then take a break**
  - We grow by stretching ourselves until we are a little uncomfortable. Try to push yourself to persevere and concentrate past when it feels easy, then take a break. Come back to work again in a few minutes.
  - Reward yourself when you know you've persevered past your comfort zone.

SKILL BUILDER

INVENTORY

CHALLENGE: Are you a person who easily gets distracted while you are trying to concentrate? What kinds of things distract you? Are you more visually distracted (you can't help but notice and look at things around you)? Audially distracted (it's hard to tune out sounds)? As you work the next couple of days, when you are off-task take note of what is distracting you. Record the distraction, the type of distraction (see the list of internal and external distractions on the previous page), and an idea of something you could try to control the distraction next time. After you try your solution, note whether it worked in the last column. If it didn't, come up with a new idea to try next time!

DISTRACTION	TYPE	SOLUTION	RESULT

Rate Your Skills and Watch Your Growth

I notice when I'm distracted. ☆ ☆ ☆ ☆ ☆

I can tell what's distracting me. ☆ ☆ ☆ ☆ ☆

I try solutions and can do things to decrease my distractions. ☆ ☆ ☆ ☆ ☆

📅 Week of ___/___/___

Reflect on the Past Week

_____

_____

_____

📅 Weekly Overview 📅

Monday	Tuesday	Wednesday

Thursday	Friday	Saturday
		Sunday

Set an Intention for the Week Ahead

_____

_____

_____

Priority Matrix

URGENT	IMPORTANT

NEEDS DONE	WOULD BE NICE

Habit Tracker

_____ ☐☐☐☐☐☐☐☐☐☐☐☐☐

_____ ☐☐☐☐☐☐☐☐☐☐☐☐☐

_____ ☐☐☐☐☐☐☐☐☐☐☐☐☐

_____ ☐☐☐☐☐☐☐☐☐☐☐☐☐

 # MONDAY ___/___/___

★ Priority Tasks

1. _____
⏳ ☐ ◯◯◯◯◯ ☐

2. _____
⏳ ☐ ◯◯◯◯◯ ☐

3. _____
⏳ ☐ ◯◯◯◯◯ ☐

✓ Additional Tasks

1. _____
⏳ ☐ ◯◯◯◯◯ ☐

2. _____
⏳ ☐ ◯◯◯◯◯ ☐

Daily Plan

6am	
7am	
8am	
9am	
10am	
11am	
12pm	
1pm	
2pm	
3pm	
4pm	
5pm	
6pm	
7pm	
8pm	

 Strategy Toolbox

- Task Inventory
- Priority Matrix
- 4th Dimension Planning
- Self-Reward
- Chunking
- Flow Sessions
- Temptation Bundling
- _____
- _____

Mood Monitor

Rate Your Day

 # TUESDAY ___/___/___

★ Priority Tasks

1. _____

⏳ ☐ ⬭⬭⬭⬭⬭ ☐

2. _____

⏳ ☐ ⬭⬭⬭⬭⬭ ☐

3. _____

⏳ ☐ ⬭⬭⬭⬭⬭ ☐

✓ Additional Tasks

1. _____

⏳ ☐ ⬭⬭⬭⬭⬭ ☐

2. _____

⏳ ☐ ⬭⬭⬭⬭⬭ ☐

🛠 Strategy Toolbox

- Task Inventory
- Priority Matrix
- 4th Dimension Planning
- Self-Reward
- Chunking
- Flow Sessions
- Temptation Bundling
- _____
- _____

Daily Plan
6am
7am
8am
9am
10am
11am
12pm
1pm
2pm
3pm
4pm
5pm
6pm
7pm
8pm

Mood Monitor

☆☆☆☆☆
Rate Your Day

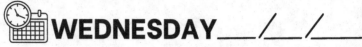

WEDNESDAY ___/___/___

★ Priority Tasks

1. _____

⏳ ☐ ⓞⓞⓞⓞⓞ ☐

2. _____

⏳ ☐ ⓞⓞⓞⓞⓞ ☐

3. _____

⏳ ☐ ⓞⓞⓞⓞⓞ ☐

✓ Additional Tasks

1. _____

⏳ ☐ ⓞⓞⓞⓞⓞ ☐

2. _____

⏳ ☐ ⓞⓞⓞⓞⓞ ☐

🛠 Strategy Toolbox

- Task Inventory
- Priority Matrix
- 4th Dimension Planning
- Self-Reward
- Chunking
- Flow Sessions
- Temptation Bundling
- _____
- _____

Daily Plan

6am	
7am	
8am	
9am	
10am	
11am	
12pm	
1pm	
2pm	
3pm	
4pm	
5pm	
6pm	
7pm	
8pm	

Mood Monitor

Rate Your Day

 **THURSDAY** ___/___/___

★ Priority Tasks

1. _____

⏳ ☐ ⦿⦿⦿⦿⦿ ☐

2. _____

⏳ ☐ ⦿⦿⦿⦿⦿ ☐

3. _____

⏳ ☐ ⦿⦿⦿⦿⦿ ☐

✓ Additional Tasks

1. _____

⏳ ☐ ⦿⦿⦿⦿⦿ ☐

2. _____

⏳ ☐ ⦿⦿⦿⦿⦿ ☐

🛠 Strategy Toolbox

- Task Inventory
- Priority Matrix
- 4th Dimension Planning
- Self-Reward
- Chunking
- Flow Sessions
- Temptation Bundling
- _____
- _____

Daily Plan
6am
7am
8am
9am
10am
11am
12pm
1pm
2pm
3pm
4pm
5pm
6pm
7pm
8pm

Mood Monitor

☆☆☆☆☆
Rate Your Day

 **FRIDAY** ___/___/___

★ Priority Tasks

1. _____

⧗ [ ] ⬯⬯⬯⬯⬯ [ ]

2. _____

⧗ [ ] ⬯⬯⬯⬯⬯ [ ]

3. _____

⧗ [ ] ⬯⬯⬯⬯⬯ [ ]

✓ Additional Tasks

1. _____

⧗ [ ] ⬯⬯⬯⬯⬯ [ ]

2. _____

⧗ [ ] ⬯⬯⬯⬯⬯ [ ]

🛠 Strategy Toolbox

- Task Inventory
- Priority Matrix
- 4th Dimension Planning
- Self-Reward
- Chunking
- Flow Sessions
- Temptation Bundling
- _ _ _ _ _ _ _ _ _ _ _ _
- _ _ _ _ _ _ _ _ _ _ _ _

Daily Plan
6am
7am
8am
9am
10am
11am
12pm
1pm
2pm
3pm
4pm
5pm
6pm
7pm
8pm

Mood Monitor

Rate Your Day

 **SATURDAY** ___/___/___

★ Priority Tasks

1. _____
   ⏳ ☐ ⦾⦾⦾⦾⦾ ☐

2. _____
   ⏳ ☐ ⦾⦾⦾⦾⦾ ☐

3. _____
   ⏳ ☐ ⦾⦾⦾⦾⦾ ☐

✓ Additional Tasks

1. _____
   ⏳ ☐ ⦾⦾⦾⦾⦾ ☐

2. _____
   ⏳ ☐ ⦾⦾⦾⦾⦾ ☐

🛠 Strategy Toolbox

- Task Inventory
- Priority Matrix
- 4th Dimension Planning
- Self-Reward
- Chunking
- Flow Sessions
- Temptation Bundling
- _____
- _____

Daily Plan

6am	
7am	
8am	
9am	
10am	
11am	
12pm	
1pm	
2pm	
3pm	
4pm	
5pm	
6pm	
7pm	
8pm	

Mood Monitor

Rate Your Day

 **SUNDAY** __ / __ / __

★ Priority Tasks

1. _____
   ⧗ [ ] ⬡⬡⬡⬡⬡ [ ]

2. _____
   ⧗ [ ] ⬡⬡⬡⬡⬡ [ ]

3. _____
   ⧗ [ ] ⬡⬡⬡⬡⬡ [ ]

✓ Additional Tasks

1. _____
   ⧗ [ ] ⬡⬡⬡⬡⬡ [ ]

2. _____
   ⧗ [ ] ⬡⬡⬡⬡⬡ [ ]

Daily Plan
6am
7am
8am
9am
10am
11am
12pm
1pm
2pm
3pm
4pm
5pm
6pm
7pm
8pm

🛠 Strategy Toolbox

- Task Inventory
- Priority Matrix
- 4th Dimension Planning
- Self-Reward
- Chunking
- Flow Sessions
- Temptation Bundling
- _____
- _____

Mood Monitor

☆☆☆☆☆
Rate Your Day

Concentration & Self-Regulation

What is the difference between concentration and self-regulation?

Concentration is staying focused on an activity outside of yourself, such as a school assignment or chore.

Self-regulation is staying focused inside your body by controlling feelings, impulses, and desires and ignoring distractions to meet a goal your brain knows is a priority.

The highest level of focus we can hope to achieve during a task is called **FLOW**. Flow is when we don't even feel the passage of time. We are so absorbed in our task that we are surprised when we look up and see that an hour or two has passed. We are operating at a higher level. Our brain recognizes how hard we are trying to concentrate and releases chemicals that help us do our best work.

Achieving **flow** requires both self-regulation AND concentration. We must push aside distracting thoughts and sensory information. We may need to control an urge to daydream or fidget. We are determined to stay focused on a challenging task. But once we settle in to concentration, it becomes easier and we tune out these distractions.

Most often, we first experience flow during activities we love, like an art project or a sport. However, we can train ourselves to be able to find the power of flow at-will, even for less-preferred tasks.

The process of getting ourselves into flow isn't always pleasant at first, but gets easier with practice. **Before completing the self-rating below, read the next page to learn about the 4 stages of flow.**

Rate Your Skills and Watch Your Growth

I understand why it's important to push through the struggle phase of flow. ☆ ☆ ☆ ☆ ☆

I can push myself through the struggle phase.
☆ ☆ ☆ ☆ ☆

I can find flow on purpose, even with less-preferred tasks. ☆ ☆ ☆ ☆ ☆

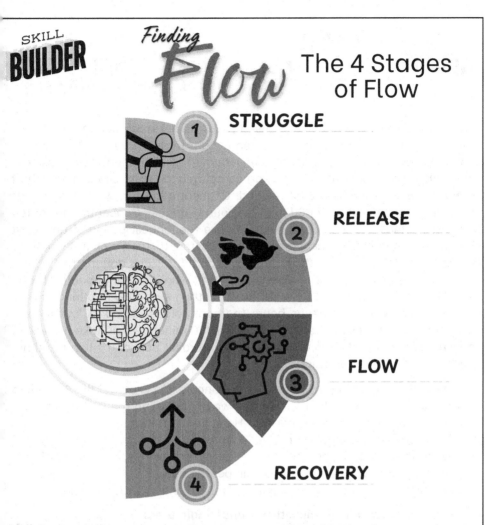

SKILL BUILDER
Finding Flow — The 4 Stages of Flow

STRUGGLE 1

RELEASE 2

FLOW 3

RECOVERY 4

1. **Struggle Phase**: When we start doing something big, hard, or complex, our brain feels overloaded and releases stress hormones. We may feel frustrated. However, we have to push through this phase–it will pass.
2. **Release Phase:** We accept that we are going to stick with this hard work, and let go of the fight against it. Our brain rewards us with some feel-good chemicals.
3. **Flow Phase:** This is where the magic happens. Time passes without us feeling it. We are absorbed in what we are doing, concentrating more easily and working more effectively. We have more access and activation of really useful areas of our brains.
4. **Recovery Phase**: Our brain is operating at a higher level and using a lot of energy during flow, so as we come out of flow we need to recover. Our brains release chemicals that relax and rejuvinate us, as well as increasing neuroplacticity (which means we learn better, locking away the benefits of what we just experienced).

Timers and Flow Sessions

We have learned that staying focused helps us get more done in less time. While that sounds simple, it can be really hard to do. As we are building our concentration skills, one strategy is to set small goals, called "flow sessions" in which we are committed to staying completely on task, and taking a short break between each session if needed. Concentrating for two hours sounds daunting. Concentrating for 30 minutes sounds doable. Concentrating for ten minutes sounds like a piece of cake. Choose the longest period of time that you think you could be successful with, and start there. It's ok if it's only 15 minutes at first. Our perceptions are valid, and if it FEELS daunting to us, our brain will struggle against it. We have to find what we are capable of, and slowly stretch ourselves. We might dread getting started with a long project when we know it will take us hours (perhaps folding laundry), but if I tell myself I will just focus on folding laundry for 10 minutes, then take a break, it doesn't seem so bad. Often, starting is the hardest part and when my timer goes off I decide to keep going.

One technique for using flow sessions to concentrate is called the **Pomodoro Technique.** In the Pomodoro Technique, we use a timing method to train our brains to stay on task for short periods. Here are the steps:
1. Set a timer for 25 minutes and get to work.
2. When the buzzer sounds, take a 5 minute break (move, take a bite of your snack, go out for a breath of fresh air, pet the dog...)
3. Set the timer for 25 minutes again and repeat until the task is done.

The circles between the hypothesis and result times for each task each represent a flow session, and together they form a "Concentration Chain" made of short times of focus with brief breaks in between if needed. As you begin, each circle might be worth ten minutes. As you grow, each circle might be worth 30 minutes. You can color in a circle each time you complete a flow session.

Rate Your Skills and Watch Your Growth

I can use a timer to concentrate for short periods, even when I don't feel like it. ☆ ☆ ☆ ☆ ☆

I can use a timer to concentrate for longer periods, even when I don't feel like it. ☆ ☆ ☆ ☆ ☆

I can concentrate for a given period of time that is a "personal best", even without a timer. ☆ ☆ ☆ ☆ ☆

📅 Week of ___/___/___

Reflect on the Past Week

_____

_____

_____

📅 Weekly Overview 📅

Monday	Tuesday	Wednesday

Thursday	Friday	Saturday

Sunday

Set an Intention for the Week Ahead

_____

_____

_____

Priority Matrix

URGENT	IMPORTANT

NEEDS DONE	WOULD BE NICE

_____

_____

_____

_____

Habit Tracker

_____ ☐☐☐☐☐☐☐☐☐☐☐☐☐☐

_____ ☐☐☐☐☐☐☐☐☐☐☐☐☐☐

_____ ☐☐☐☐☐☐☐☐☐☐☐☐☐☐

_____ ☐☐☐☐☐☐☐☐☐☐☐☐☐☐

 **MONDAY** ___/___/___

★ Priority Tasks

1. _____

 ☐ ⦿⦿⦿⦿⦿ ☐

2. _____

☐ ⦿⦿⦿⦿⦿ ☐

3. _____

☐ ⦿⦿⦿⦿⦿ ☐

✓ Additional Tasks

1. _____

☐ ⦿⦿⦿⦿⦿ ☐

2. _____

☐ ⦿⦿⦿⦿⦿ ☐

🛠️ Strategy Toolbox

- Task Inventory
- Priority Matrix
- 4th Dimension Planning
- Self-Reward
- Chunking
- Flow Sessions
- Temptation Bundling
- _____
- _____

Daily Plan
6am
7am
8am
9am
10am
11am
12pm
1pm
2pm
3pm
4pm
5pm
6pm
7pm
8pm

Mood Monitor

Rate Your Day

 # TUESDAY ___/___/___

★ Priority Tasks

1. _____

⏳ ☐ ⬭⬭⬭⬭⬭ ☐

2. _____

⏳ ☐ ⬭⬭⬭⬭⬭ ☐

3. _____

⏳ ☐ ⬭⬭⬭⬭⬭ ☐

✓ Additional Tasks

1. _____

⏳ ☐ ⬭⬭⬭⬭⬭ ☐

2. _____

⏳ ☐ ⬭⬭⬭⬭⬭ ☐

🛠 Strategy Toolbox

- Task Inventory
- Priority Matrix
- 4th Dimension Planning
- Self-Reward
- Chunking
- Flow Sessions
- Temptation Bundling
- _____
- _____

Daily Plan
6am
7am
8am
9am
10am
11am
12pm
1pm
2pm
3pm
4pm
5pm
6pm
7pm
8pm

Mood Monitor

Rate Your Day

 # WEDNESDAY ___/___/___

★ Priority Tasks

1. _____
⧖ ☐ ◯◯◯◯◯ ☐

2. _____
⧖ ☐ ◯◯◯◯◯ ☐

3. _____
⧖ ☐ ◯◯◯◯◯ ☐

✓ Additional Tasks

1. _____
⧖ ☐ ◯◯◯◯◯ ☐

2. _____
⧖ ☐ ◯◯◯◯◯ ☐

Daily Plan

Time
6am
7am
8am
9am
10am
11am
12pm
1pm
2pm
3pm
4pm
5pm
6pm
7pm
8pm

🛠 Strategy Toolbox

- Task Inventory
- Priority Matrix
- 4th Dimension Planning
- Self-Reward
- Chunking
- Flow Sessions
- Temptation Bundling
- _____
- _____

Mood Monitor

Rate Your Day

THURSDAY ___/___/___

★ Priority Tasks

1. _____
   ⏳ [ ] ◯◯◯◯◯ [ ]

2. _____
   ⏳ [ ] ◯◯◯◯◯ [ ]

3. _____
   ⏳ [ ] ◯◯◯◯◯ [ ]

✓ Additional Tasks

1. _____
   ⏳ [ ] ◯◯◯◯◯ [ ]

2. _____
   ⏳ [ ] ◯◯◯◯◯ [ ]

 Strategy Toolbox

- Task Inventory
- Priority Matrix
- 4th Dimension Planning
- Self-Reward
- Chunking
- Flow Sessions
- Temptation Bundling
- _____
- _____

Daily Plan
6am
7am
8am
9am
10am
11am
12pm
1pm
2pm
3pm
4pm
5pm
6pm
7pm
8pm

Mood Monitor

Rate Your Day

 **FRIDAY** __ / __ / __

★ Priority Tasks

1. _____
⏳ ☐ ⬡⬡⬡⬡⬡ ☐

2. _____
⏳ ☐ ⬡⬡⬡⬡⬡ ☐

3. _____
⏳ ☐ ⬡⬡⬡⬡⬡ ☐

✓ Additional Tasks

1. _____
⏳ ☐ ⬡⬡⬡⬡⬡ ☐

2. _____
⏳ ☐ ⬡⬡⬡⬡⬡ ☐

🛠 Strategy Toolbox

- Task Inventory
- Priority Matrix
- 4th Dimension Planning
- Self-Reward
- Chunking
- Flow Sessions
- Temptation Bundling
- _____
- _____

Daily Plan
6am
7am
8am
9am
10am
11am
12pm
1pm
2pm
3pm
4pm
5pm
6pm
7pm
8pm

Mood Monitor

Rate Your Day

 **SATURDAY** ___/___/___

★ Priority Tasks

1. _____

⏳ ☐ ○○○○○ ☐

2. _____

⏳ ☐ ○○○○○ ☐

3. _____

⏳ ☐ ○○○○○ ☐

✓ Additional Tasks

1. _____

⏳ ☐ ○○○○○ ☐

2. _____

⏳ ☐ ○○○○○ ☐

🛠 Strategy Toolbox

- Task Inventory
- Priority Matrix
- 4th Dimension Planning
- Self-Reward
- Chunking
- Flow Sessions
- Temptation Bundling
- _____
- _____

Daily Plan
6am
7am
8am
9am
10am
11am
12pm
1pm
2pm
3pm
4pm
5pm
6pm
7pm
8pm

Mood Monitor

Rate Your Day

 **SUNDAY** ___/___/___

★ Priority Tasks

1. _____

⏳ ☐ ◯◯◯◯◯ ☐

2. _____

⏳ ☐ ◯◯◯◯◯ ☐

3. _____

⏳ ☐ ◯◯◯◯◯ ☐

✓ Additional Tasks

1. _____

⏳ ☐ ◯◯◯◯◯ ☐

2. _____

⏳ ☐ ◯◯◯◯◯ ☐

 Strategy Toolbox

- Task Inventory
- Priority Matrix
- 4th Dimension Planning
- Self-Reward
- Chunking
- Flow Sessions
- Temptation Bundling
- _____
- _____

Daily Plan

Time	
6am	
7am	
8am	
9am	
10am	
11am	
12pm	
1pm	
2pm	
3pm	
4pm	
5pm	
6pm	
7pm	
8pm	

Mood Monitor

Rate Your Day

BUILDING STRONG

Habits

Habits are behaviors we repeat regularly. They become easier and more automatic the more we do them. To build a habit, start small so that you can be successful. Be patient and visualize your goals. For this planner, let's focus on the strategies that have worked for you or the routines that seem effective for getting tasks done. For example, is it more effective for you to look at your planner and organize your day in the morning when you sit at your desk? Or the night before as you are getting ready to leave and thinking about where you will need to pick back up tomorrow? If you try both and the morning seems to work better, then perhaps you want to build a habit of using your planner when you start each day.

Or perhaps you have found that taking a break to eat a small snack, such as a slice of apple, helps you with your concentration chain? Then a habit you may want to build is to prepare a snack box each morning to take with you. What is working for you? If you're not sure, first do some action research, then determine some habits you would like to build. The week overview has a habit tracker (like the one below) for you to self-monitor your progress by marking how many times you practice a habit. Below the example, think at least one habit you would like to try and track it for a few days.

Habit Tracker

Go for walk before p.m. work time ● ● ● ● ● ● ● □ □ □ □ □ □ □

_____ □ □ □ □ □ □ □ □ □ □ □ □ □ □

_____ □ □ □ □ □ □ □ □ □ □ □ □ □ □

_____ □ □ □ □ □ □ □ □ □ □ □ □ □ □

Rate Your Skills and Watch Your Growth

I can identify habits that would help me get things done. ☆ ☆ ☆ ☆ ☆

I can regularly remember to do the behaviors I am trying to build. ☆ ☆ ☆ ☆ ☆

Habits feel easier with practice. ☆ ☆ ☆ ☆ ☆

📅 Week of ___/___/___

Reflect on the Past Week

_____

_____

_____

📅 Weekly Overview 📅

Monday	Tuesday	Wednesday

Thursday	Friday	Saturday
		Sunday

Set an Intention for the Week Ahead

_____

_____

_____

Priority Matrix

URGENT	IMPORTANT

NEEDS DONE	WOULD BE NICE

Habit Tracker

_____ ☐☐☐☐☐☐☐☐☐☐☐☐

_____ ☐☐☐☐☐☐☐☐☐☐☐☐

_____ ☐☐☐☐☐☐☐☐☐☐☐☐

_____ ☐☐☐☐☐☐☐☐☐☐☐☐

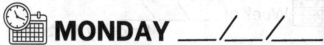 # MONDAY ___/___/___

★ Priority Tasks

1. _____
   ⏳ ☐ ⃝⃝⃝⃝⃝ ☐

2. _____
   ⏳ ☐ ⃝⃝⃝⃝⃝ ☐

3. _____
   ⏳ ☐ ⃝⃝⃝⃝⃝ ☐

✓ Additional Tasks

1. _____
   ⏳ ☐ ⃝⃝⃝⃝⃝ ☐

2. _____
   ⏳ ☐ ⃝⃝⃝⃝⃝ ☐

🛠 Strategy Toolbox

- Task Inventory
- Priority Matrix
- 4th Dimension Planning
- Self-Reward
- Chunking
- Flow Sessions
- Temptation Bundling
- _____
- _____

Daily Plan
6am
7am
8am
9am
10am
11am
12pm
1pm
2pm
3pm
4pm
5pm
6pm
7pm
8pm

Mood Monitor

Rate Your Day

# TUESDAY ___/___/___

★ Priority Tasks

1. _____
⧗ ☐ ⵔⵔⵔⵔⵔ ☐

2. _____
⧗ ☐ ⵔⵔⵔⵔⵔ ☐

3. _____
⧗ ☐ ⵔⵔⵔⵔⵔ ☐

✓ Additional Tasks

1. _____
⧗ ☐ ⵔⵔⵔⵔⵔ ☐

2. _____
⧗ ☐ ⵔⵔⵔⵔⵔ ☐

Daily Plan

| 6am |
| 7am |
| 8am |
| 9am |
| 10am |
| 11am |
| 12pm |
| 1pm |
| 2pm |
| 3pm |
| 4pm |
| 5pm |
| 6pm |
| 7pm |
| 8pm |

**Strategy Toolbox**

- Task Inventory
- Priority Matrix
- 4th Dimension Planning
- Self-Reward
- Chunking
- Flow Sessions
- Temptation Bundling
- _____
- _____

Mood Monitor

☆☆☆☆☆
Rate Your Day

 **WEDNESDAY** ___/___/___

★ Priority Tasks

1._____
⏳ ☐ ◯◯◯◯◯ ☐

2._____
⏳ ☐ ◯◯◯◯◯ ☐

3._____
⏳ ☐ ◯◯◯◯◯ ☐

✓ Additional Tasks

1._____
⏳ ☐ ◯◯◯◯◯ ☐

2._____
⏳ ☐ ◯◯◯◯◯ ☐

Daily Plan

6am	
7am	
8am	
9am	
10am	
11am	
12pm	
1pm	
2pm	
3pm	
4pm	
5pm	
6pm	
7pm	
8pm	

 Strategy Toolbox
- Task Inventory
- Priority Matrix
- 4th Dimension Planning
- Self-Reward
- Chunking
- Flow Sessions
- Temptation Bundling
- _____
- _____

Mood Monitor

Rate Your Day

⏰📅 THURSDAY ___/___/___

★ Priority Tasks

1. _____
⏳ ☐ ◯◯◯◯◯ ☐

2. _____
⏳ ☐ ◯◯◯◯◯ ☐

3. _____
⏳ ☐ ◯◯◯◯◯ ☐

✓ Additional Tasks

1. _____
⏳ ☐ ◯◯◯◯◯ ☐

2. _____
⏳ ☐ ◯◯◯◯◯ ☐

🛠️ Strategy Toolbox

- Task Inventory
- Priority Matrix
- 4th Dimension Planning
- Self-Reward
- Chunking
- Flow Sessions
- Temptation Bundling
- _____
- _____

Daily Plan
6am
7am
8am
9am
10am
11am
12pm
1pm
2pm
3pm
4pm
5pm
6pm
7pm
8pm

Mood Monitor

Rate Your Day

 **FRIDAY** ___/___/___

★ Priority Tasks

Daily Plan

1. _____

⌛ ☐ ⵔⵔⵔⵔⵔ ☐

2. _____

⌛ ☐ ⵔⵔⵔⵔⵔ ☐

3. _____

⌛ ☐ ⵔⵔⵔⵔⵔ ☐

✓ Additional Tasks

1. _____

⌛ ☐ ⵔⵔⵔⵔⵔ ☐

2. _____

⌛ ☐ ⵔⵔⵔⵔⵔ ☐

Daily Plan

6am
7am
8am
9am
10am
11am
12pm
1pm
2pm
3pm
4pm
5pm
6pm
7pm
8pm

 Strategy Toolbox

- Task Inventory
- Priority Matrix
- 4th Dimension Planning
- Self-Reward
- Chunking
- Flow Sessions
- Temptation Bundling
- _____
- _____

Mood Monitor

Rate Your Day

🕐📅 SATURDAY __/__/__

★ Priority Tasks

1. _____

⏳ ☐ ◯◯◯◯◯ ☐

2. _____

⏳ ☐ ◯◯◯◯◯ ☐

3. _____

⏳ ☐ ◯◯◯◯◯ ☐

✓ Additional Tasks

1. _____

⏳ ☐ ◯◯◯◯◯ ☐

2. _____

⏳ ☐ ◯◯◯◯◯ ☐

Strategy Toolbox

- Task Inventory
- Priority Matrix
- 4th Dimension Planning
- Self-Reward
- Chunking
- Flow Sessions
- Temptation Bundling
- _____
- _____

Daily Plan
6am
7am
8am
9am
10am
11am
12pm
1pm
2pm
3pm
4pm
5pm
6pm
7pm
8pm

Mood Monitor

Rate Your Day

SUNDAY ___ / ___ / ___

★ Priority Tasks

1. _____
   ⏳ ☐ ⃝⃝⃝⃝⃝ ☐

2. _____
   ⏳ ☐ ⃝⃝⃝⃝⃝ ☐

3. _____
   ⏳ ☐ ⃝⃝⃝⃝⃝ ☐

✓ Additional Tasks

1. _____
   ⏳ ☐ ⃝⃝⃝⃝⃝ ☐

2. _____
   ⏳ ☐ ⃝⃝⃝⃝⃝ ☐

🛠 Strategy Toolbox

- Task Inventory
- Priority Matrix
- 4th Dimension Planning
- Self-Reward
- Chunking
- Flow Sessions
- Temptation Bundling
- _____
- _____

Daily Plan

Time
6am
7am
8am
9am
10am
11am
12pm
1pm
2pm
3pm
4pm
5pm
6pm
7pm
8pm

Mood Monitor

Rate Your Day

Motivation
POSITIVE REINFORCEMENT

Motivation is a person's internal drive to do something. It is the "why" behind every action. This planner is about getting things done. **Why** do you want to get things done?

Motivation is key to reaching your goals. It's the fire that keeps us pushing forward, even when things feel tough. Motivation goes up and down, though, and can be impacted by factors such as our mood, sleep, nutrition, etc.

So how do we help ourselves find motivation when it's not coming to us naturally? Well, there are some evidence-based tips that might help us.

Positive Reinforcement is when we get something for doing something. If someone threw you a piece of candy every time you completed a task, you would probably begin to complete more tasks. However, you would begin to complete tasks for *them*, not for *you.* This is called "extrinsic motivation". A healthier form of motivation is "intrinsic motivation", where we are responsible for ourselves and our own happiness, and are not performing to make others happy.

Does that mean you don't get a treat? No! We can reward *ourselves*. We can set goals for ourselves, and also decide what "treat" we will give ourselves when we reach the goal. These self-chosen rewards can be personalized to you. It wouldn't be very healthy to use candy all of the time, so think about other options as well such as:

- getting to play a game you'd like to once you finish your essay
- calling or texting with a friend after you've concentrated for 45 minutes
- Getting a delicious snack, setting it at your workplace for when you complete your math homework
- Watching an episode of a favorite show after you clean your room

What are some "treats" you could give yourself as rewards?

Rate Your Skills and Watch Your Growth

I can self-reward. ☆ ☆ ☆ ☆ ☆

When I self-reward, I can push through and get tasks done that I don't feel like doing. ☆ ☆ ☆ ☆ ☆

📅 Week of ___/___/___

Reflect on the Past Week

_____

_____

_____

📅 Weekly Overview 📅

Monday

Tuesday

Wednesday

Thursday

Friday

Saturday

Sunday

Set an Intention for the Week Ahead

_____

_____

_____

Priority Matrix

URGENT	IMPORTANT
NEEDS DONE	**WOULD BE NICE**

_____

_____

_____

_____

Habit Tracker

_____ ☐☐☐☐☐☐☐☐☐☐☐☐☐☐

_____ ☐☐☐☐☐☐☐☐☐☐☐☐☐☐

_____ ☐☐☐☐☐☐☐☐☐☐☐☐☐☐

_____ ☐☐☐☐☐☐☐☐☐☐☐☐☐☐

 **MONDAY** ___/___/___

★ Priority Tasks

1. _____
 ☐ ⃝⃝⃝⃝⃝ ☐

2. _____
☐ ⃝⃝⃝⃝⃝ ☐

3. _____
☐ ⃝⃝⃝⃝⃝ ☐

✓ Additional Tasks

1. _____
☐ ⃝⃝⃝⃝⃝ ☐

2. _____
☐ ⃝⃝⃝⃝⃝ ☐

✗ Strategy Toolbox

- Task Inventory
- Priority Matrix
- 4th Dimension Planning
- Self-Reward
- Chunking
- Flow Sessions
- Temptation Bundling
- _____
- _____

Daily Plan

6am	
7am	
8am	
9am	
10am	
11am	
12pm	
1pm	
2pm	
3pm	
4pm	
5pm	
6pm	
7pm	
8pm	

Mood Monitor

Rate Your Day

 **TUESDAY** ___/___/___

★ Priority Tasks

1. _____

⏳ ☐ ⬭⬭⬭⬭⬭ ☐

2. _____

⏳ ☐ ⬭⬭⬭⬭⬭ ☐

3. _____

⏳ ☐ ⬭⬭⬭⬭⬭ ☐

✓ Additional Tasks

1. _____

⏳ ☐ ⬭⬭⬭⬭⬭ ☐

2. _____

⏳ ☐ ⬭⬭⬭⬭⬭ ☐

Daily Plan

6am	
7am	
8am	
9am	
10am	
11am	
12pm	
1pm	
2pm	
3pm	
4pm	
5pm	
6pm	
7pm	
8pm	

Strategy Toolbox

- Task Inventory
- Priority Matrix
- 4th Dimension Planning
- Self-Reward
- Chunking
- Flow Sessions
- Temptation Bundling
- _____
- _____

Mood Monitor

Rate Your Day

 # WEDNESDAY ___/___/___

★ Priority Tasks

1. _____
   ⏳ ☐ ◯◯◯◯◯ ☐

2. _____
   ⏳ ☐ ◯◯◯◯◯ ☐

3. _____
   ⏳ ☐ ◯◯◯◯◯ ☐

✓ Additional Tasks

1. _____
   ⏳ ☐ ◯◯◯◯◯ ☐

2. _____
   ⏳ ☐ ◯◯◯◯◯ ☐

🛠 Strategy Toolbox

- Task Inventory
- Priority Matrix
- 4th Dimension Planning
- Self-Reward
- Chunking
- Flow Sessions
- Temptation Bundling
- _____
- _____

Daily Plan
6am
7am
8am
9am
10am
11am
12pm
1pm
2pm
3pm
4pm
5pm
6pm
7pm
8pm

Mood Monitor

Rate Your Day

THURSDAY ___/___/___

★ Priority Tasks

1. _____

⏳ ☐ ⚪⚪⚪⚪⚪ ☐

2. _____

⏳ ☐ ⚪⚪⚪⚪⚪ ☐

3. _____

⏳ ☐ ⚪⚪⚪⚪⚪ ☐

✓ Additional Tasks

1. _____

⏳ ☐ ⚪⚪⚪⚪⚪ ☐

2. _____

⏳ ☐ ⚪⚪⚪⚪⚪ ☐

Daily Plan

6am

7am

8am

9am

10am

11am

12pm

1pm

2pm

3pm

4pm

5pm

6pm

7pm

8pm

Strategy Toolbox

- Task Inventory
- Priority Matrix
- 4th Dimension Planning
- Self-Reward
- Chunking
- Flow Sessions
- Temptation Bundling
- _____
- _____

Mood Monitor

Rate Your Day

FRIDAY __/__/__

★ Priority Tasks

1. _____
   ⧖ ☐ ⬡⬡⬡⬡⬡ ☐

2. _____
   ⧖ ☐ ⬡⬡⬡⬡⬡ ☐

3. _____
   ⧖ ☐ ⬡⬡⬡⬡⬡ ☐

✓ Additional Tasks

1. _____
   ⧖ ☐ ⬡⬡⬡⬡⬡ ☐

2. _____
   ⧖ ☐ ⬡⬡⬡⬡⬡ ☐

Daily Plan

6am	
7am	
8am	
9am	
10am	
11am	
12pm	
1pm	
2pm	
3pm	
4pm	
5pm	
6pm	
7pm	
8pm	

Strategy Toolbox

- Task Inventory
- Priority Matrix
- 4th Dimension Planning
- Self-Reward
- Chunking
- Flow Sessions
- Temptation Bundling
- _____
- _____

Mood Monitor

Rate Your Day

📅 SATURDAY ___/___/___

★ Priority Tasks

1. _____
   ⏳ [ ] ⚪⚪⚪⚪⚪ [ ]

2. _____
   ⏳ [ ] ⚪⚪⚪⚪⚪ [ ]

3. _____
   ⏳ [ ] ⚪⚪⚪⚪⚪ [ ]

✓ Additional Tasks

1. _____
   ⏳ [ ] ⚪⚪⚪⚪⚪ [ ]

2. _____
   ⏳ [ ] ⚪⚪⚪⚪⚪ [ ]

🛠️ Strategy Toolbox

- Task Inventory
- Priority Matrix
- 4th Dimension Planning
- Self-Reward
- Chunking
- Flow Sessions
- Temptation Bundling
- _____
- _____

Daily Plan

6am
7am
8am
9am
10am
11am
12pm
1pm
2pm
3pm
4pm
5pm
6pm
7pm
8pm

Mood Monitor

Rate Your Day

142

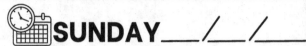

SUNDAY___/___/___

★ Priority Tasks

1. _____
   ⏳ [ ] ⬤⬤⬤⬤⬤ [ ]

2. _____
   ⏳ [ ] ⬤⬤⬤⬤⬤ [ ]

3. _____
   ⏳ [ ] ⬤⬤⬤⬤⬤ [ ]

✓ Additional Tasks

1. _____
   ⏳ [ ] ⬤⬤⬤⬤⬤ [ ]

2. _____
   ⏳ [ ] ⬤⬤⬤⬤⬤ [ ]

Daily Plan

- 6am
- 7am
- 8am
- 9am
- 10am
- 11am
- 12pm
- 1pm
- 2pm
- 3pm
- 4pm
- 5pm
- 6pm
- 7pm
- 8pm

 Strategy Toolbox

- Task Inventory
- Priority Matrix
- 4th Dimension Planning
- Self-Reward
- Chunking
- Flow Sessions
- Temptation Bundling
- _____
- _____

Mood Monitor

Rate Your Day

TEMPTATION BUNDLING

Temptation bundling is another trick to increasing motivation. **It is a productivity technique in which you pair something you don't want to do with something you like doing.** The idea is that we will associate the task we don't like with the thing we do like, and it will start to feel more appealing, increasing our motivation to do it. This is a great trick for kick-starting new habits or getting through dreaded chores.

One example I have for temptation bundling is running. For years I worked to build a running habit, but wasn't very successful. Then I tried temptation bundingly and began to listen to a comedy podcast while I ran. I didn't listen to the podcast any other time except for when I was running. In time, when I thought about going for a run, I would actually feel eager because I was excited to hear the next episode of the podcast.

I have a friend who has a fancy foot massager machine that she never takes home-it only lives under her desk at work. She can often be seen typing away, and the hum of the machine can be heard from the floor.

My youngest son liked to do his homework at the kitchen table while I baked and steal raw cookie dough to eat when he thought I wasn't looking.

What are some temptations you could bundle with your work? Perhaps you could find a good friend who also cares about doing well on the upcoming test. Study sessions together over a bowl of popcorn might give you something to look forward to.

Rate Your Skills and Watch Your Growth

I can think of some good pairs of temptations that can be bundled with tasks. ☆ ☆ ☆ ☆ ☆

I save the temptation for when I'm doing tasks and it helps me look forward to the task. ☆ ☆ ☆ ☆ ☆

📅 Week of ___/___/___

Reflect on the Past Week

_____

_____

_____

📅 Weekly Overview 📅

Monday	Tuesday	Wednesday

Thursday	Friday	Saturday
		Sunday

Set an Intention for the Week Ahead

_____

_____

_____

Priority Matrix

URGENT	IMPORTANT
NEEDS DONE	**WOULD BE NICE**

_____

_____

_____

_____

Habit Tracker

_____ ☐☐☐☐☐☐☐☐☐☐☐☐☐☐

_____ ☐☐☐☐☐☐☐☐☐☐☐☐☐☐

_____ ☐☐☐☐☐☐☐☐☐☐☐☐☐☐

_____ ☐☐☐☐☐☐☐☐☐☐☐☐☐☐

 # MONDAY ___/___/___

★ Priority Tasks

1. _____
 ⏳ [ ] ◯◯◯◯◯ [ ]

2. _____
⏳ [ ] ◯◯◯◯◯ [ ]

3. _____
⏳ [ ] ◯◯◯◯◯ [ ]

✓ Additional Tasks

1. _____
⏳ [ ] ◯◯◯◯◯ [ ]

2. _____
⏳ [ ] ◯◯◯◯◯ [ ]

🛠 Strategy Toolbox

- Task Inventory
- Priority Matrix
- 4th Dimension Planning
- Self-Reward
- Chunking
- Flow Sessions
- Temptation Bundling
- _____
- _____

Daily Plan
6am
7am
8am
9am
10am
11am
12pm
1pm
2pm
3pm
4pm
5pm
6pm
7pm
8pm

Mood Monitor

Rate Your Day

TUESDAY ___/___/___

★ Priority Tasks

1. _____

⏳ ☐ ⬭⬭⬭⬭⬭ ☐

2. _____

⏳ ☐ ⬭⬭⬭⬭⬭ ☐

3. _____

⏳ ☐ ⬭⬭⬭⬭⬭ ☐

✓ Additional Tasks

1. _____

⏳ ☐ ⬭⬭⬭⬭⬭ ☐

2. _____

⏳ ☐ ⬭⬭⬭⬭⬭ ☐

Daily Plan

6am	
7am	
8am	
9am	
10am	
11am	
12pm	
1pm	
2pm	
3pm	
4pm	
5pm	
6pm	
7pm	
8pm	

🛠 Strategy Toolbox

- Task Inventory
- Priority Matrix
- 4th Dimension Planning
- Self-Reward
- Chunking
- Flow Sessions
- Temptation Bundling
- _____
- _____

Mood Monitor

Rate Your Day

WEDNESDAY ___/___/___

★ Priority Tasks

1. _____

⏳ ☐ ◯◯◯◯◯ ☐

2. _____

⏳ ☐ ◯◯◯◯◯ ☐

3. _____

⏳ ☐ ◯◯◯◯◯ ☐

✓ Additional Tasks

1. _____

⏳ ☐ ◯◯◯◯◯ ☐

2. _____

⏳ ☐ ◯◯◯◯◯ ☐

Strategy Toolbox

- Task Inventory
- Priority Matrix
- 4th Dimension Planning
- Self-Reward
- Chunking
- Flow Sessions
- Temptation Bundling
- _____
- _____

Daily Plan

Time	
6am	
7am	
8am	
9am	
10am	
11am	
12pm	
1pm	
2pm	
3pm	
4pm	
5pm	
6pm	
7pm	
8pm	

Mood Monitor

Rate Your Day

⏰📅 THURSDAY ___/___/___

★ Priority Tasks

1. _____

⏳ ☐ ⃝⃝⃝⃝⃝ ☐

2. _____

⏳ ☐ ⃝⃝⃝⃝⃝ ☐

3. _____

⏳ ☐ ⃝⃝⃝⃝⃝ ☐

✓ Additional Tasks

1. _____

⏳ ☐ ⃝⃝⃝⃝⃝ ☐

2. _____

⏳ ☐ ⃝⃝⃝⃝⃝ ☐

Daily Plan
6am
7am
8am
9am
10am
11am
12pm
1pm
2pm
3pm
4pm
5pm
6pm
7pm
8pm

Strategy Toolbox

- Task Inventory
- Priority Matrix
- 4th Dimension Planning
- Self-Reward
- Chunking
- Flow Sessions
- Temptation Bundling
- _____
- _____

Mood Monitor

Rate Your Day

 **FRIDAY** ___/___/___

★ Priority Tasks

1. _____

⏳ ☐ ⊙⊙⊙⊙⊙ ☐

2. _____

⏳ ☐ ⊙⊙⊙⊙⊙ ☐

3. _____

⏳ ☐ ⊙⊙⊙⊙⊙ ☐

✓ Additional Tasks

1. _____

⏳ ☐ ⊙⊙⊙⊙⊙ ☐

2. _____

⏳ ☐ ⊙⊙⊙⊙⊙ ☐

Daily Plan

Time	
6am	
7am	
8am	
9am	
10am	
11am	
12pm	
1pm	
2pm	
3pm	
4pm	
5pm	
6pm	
7pm	
8pm	

 Strategy Toolbox

- Task Inventory
- Priority Matrix
- 4th Dimension Planning
- Self-Reward
- Chunking
- Flow Sessions
- Temptation Bundling
- _____
- _____

Mood Monitor

Rate Your Day

SATURDAY___/___/___

★ Priority Tasks

1. _____

⧗ ☐ ◯◯◯◯◯ ☐

2. _____

⧗ ☐ ◯◯◯◯◯ ☐

3. _____

⧗ ☐ ◯◯◯◯◯ ☐

✓ Additional Tasks

1. _____

⧗ ☐ ◯◯◯◯◯ ☐

2. _____

⧗ ☐ ◯◯◯◯◯ ☐

Daily Plan

6am	
7am	
8am	
9am	
10am	
11am	
12pm	
1pm	
2pm	
3pm	
4pm	
5pm	
6pm	
7pm	
8pm	

 Strategy Toolbox

- Task Inventory
- Priority Matrix
- 4th Dimension Planning
- Self-Reward
- Chunking
- Flow Sessions
- Temptation Bundling
- _____
- _____

Mood Monitor

Rate Your Day

 **SUNDAY** __/__/__

★ Priority Tasks

1. _____

⧖ ☐ ◯◯◯◯◯ ☐

2. _____

⧖ ☐ ◯◯◯◯◯ ☐

3. _____

⧖ ☐ ◯◯◯◯◯ ☐

✓ Additional Tasks

1. _____

⧖ ☐ ◯◯◯◯◯ ☐

2. _____

⧖ ☐ ◯◯◯◯◯ ☐

Daily Plan
6am
7am
8am
9am
10am
11am
12pm
1pm
2pm
3pm
4pm
5pm
6pm
7pm
8pm

 Strategy Toolbox

- Task Inventory
- Priority Matrix
- 4th Dimension Planning
- Self-Reward
- Chunking
- Flow Sessions
- Temptation Bundling
- _____
- _____

Mood Monitor

Rate Your Day

THE SNOWBALL EFFECT

This last motivation technique actually breaks a couple of the guidelines we've talked about so far, but it can be an important tool in certain situations.

Let's imagine that the number one task on your urgent list is something so large or hard or overwhelming, that even breaking it down into chunks is not enough. You've tried to focus on it, and have lost a lot of time "stuck". You aren't getting enough done to feel like you are successfully moving forward, and you don't have a strategy that feels like it will fix the problem.

That's where the snowball effect comes in. Sometimes we just need a win. We need to feel like we are making progress. So, we start with something small.

Picture rolling a snowball down a mountain. As it picks up more snow it gets bigger and bigger. By the bottom of the mountain, it is a snow boulder. The snowball effect method uses this idea of small things adding up. It is often associated with debts, where a person might pay off several small debts to feel good and get a start instead of tackling one giant overwhelming debt.

When you need a win and are feeling stuck, sometimes it can make sense to pause on your big (and most urgent) task and instead look at your list for a couple of quick and easy items you can check off right away. Finishing these small items can give you a reset and a boost of confidence to turn back to the task you are stuck on. However, it's important to be able to tell the difference between using the snowball effect to reset yourself, and just picking the easy things off your list because you're avoiding something harder that you really should be doing.

📅 Week of ___/___/___

Reflect on the Past Week

📅 Weekly Overview 📅

Monday	Tuesday	Wednesday

Thursday	Friday	Saturday
		Sunday

Set an Intention for the Week Ahead

Priority Matrix

URGENT	IMPORTANT

NEEDS DONE	WOULD BE NICE

Habit Tracker

□□□□□□□□□□□□□□

□□□□□□□□□□□□□□

□□□□□□□□□□□□□□

□□□□□□□□□□□□□□

 **MONDAY** ___/___/___

★ Priority Tasks

1._____
⧗ [ ] ⭕⭕⭕⭕⭕ [ ]

2._____
⧗ [ ] ⭕⭕⭕⭕⭕ [ ]

3._____
⧗ [ ] ⭕⭕⭕⭕⭕ [ ]

✓ Additional Tasks

1._____
⧗ [ ] ⭕⭕⭕⭕⭕ [ ]

2._____
⧗ [ ] ⭕⭕⭕⭕⭕ [ ]

🛠 Strategy Toolbox

- Task Inventory
- Priority Matrix
- 4th Dimension Planning
- Self-Reward
- Chunking
- Flow Sessions
- Temptation Bundling
- _____
- _____

Daily Plan
6am
7am
8am
9am
10am
11am
12pm
1pm
2pm
3pm
4pm
5pm
6pm
7pm
8pm

Mood Monitor

Rate Your Day

 # TUESDAY ___ / ___ / ___

★ Priority Tasks

1. _____
⧗ ☐ ○○○○○ ☐

2. _____
⧗ ☐ ○○○○○ ☐

3. _____
⧗ ☐ ○○○○○ ☐

✓ Additional Tasks

1. _____
⧗ ☐ ○○○○○ ☐

2. _____
⧗ ☐ ○○○○○ ☐

🛠 Strategy Toolbox

- Task Inventory
- Priority Matrix
- 4th Dimension Planning
- Self-Reward
- Chunking
- Flow Sessions
- Temptation Bundling
- _____
- _____

Daily Plan
6am
7am
8am
9am
10am
11am
12pm
1pm
2pm
3pm
4pm
5pm
6pm
7pm
8pm

Mood Monitor

Rate Your Day

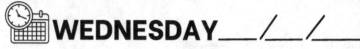 # WEDNESDAY___/___/___

★ Priority Tasks

1._____

⏳ ☐ ◯◯◯◯◯ ☐

2._____

⏳ ☐ ◯◯◯◯◯ ☐

3._____

⏳ ☐ ◯◯◯◯◯ ☐

✓ Additional Tasks

1._____

⏳ ☐ ◯◯◯◯◯ ☐

2._____

⏳ ☐ ◯◯◯◯◯ ☐

 Strategy Toolbox

- Task Inventory
- Priority Matrix
- 4th Dimension Planning
- Self-Reward
- Chunking
- Flow Sessions
- Temptation Bundling
- _____
- _____

Daily Plan
6am
7am
8am
9am
10am
11am
12pm
1pm
2pm
3pm
4pm
5pm
6pm
7pm
8pm

Mood Monitor

Rate Your Day

THURSDAY ___/___/___

★ Priority Tasks

1. _____
⏳ ☐ ⟨○○○○○⟩ ☐

2. _____
⏳ ☐ ⟨○○○○○⟩ ☐

3. _____
⏳ ☐ ⟨○○○○○⟩ ☐

✓ Additional Tasks

1. _____
⏳ ☐ ⟨○○○○○⟩ ☐

2. _____
⏳ ☐ ⟨○○○○○⟩ ☐

🛠 Strategy Toolbox

- Task Inventory
- Priority Matrix
- 4th Dimension Planning
- Self-Reward
- Chunking
- Flow Sessions
- Temptation Bundling
- _____
- _____

Daily Plan

6am
7am
8am
9am
10am
11am
12pm
1pm
2pm
3pm
4pm
5pm
6pm
7pm
8pm

Mood Monitor

Rate Your Day

FRIDAY___/___/___

★ Priority Tasks

1. _____

⏳ ☐ ⬭⬭⬭⬭⬭ ☐

2. _____

⏳ ☐ ⬭⬭⬭⬭⬭ ☐

3. _____

⏳ ☐ ⬭⬭⬭⬭⬭ ☐

✓ Additional Tasks

1. _____

⏳ ☐ ⬭⬭⬭⬭⬭ ☐

2. _____

⏳ ☐ ⬭⬭⬭⬭⬭ ☐

Daily Plan
6am
7am
8am
9am
10am
11am
12pm
1pm
2pm
3pm
4pm
5pm
6pm
7pm
8pm

🛠 Strategy Toolbox

- Task Inventory
- Priority Matrix
- 4th Dimension Planning
- Self-Reward
- Chunking
- Flow Sessions
- Temptation Bundling
- _____
- _____

Mood Monitor

Rate Your Day

⏰📅 SATURDAY ___/___/___

★ Priority Tasks

1. _____

⏳ ☐ ○○○○○ ☐

2. _____

⏳ ☐ ○○○○○ ☐

3. _____

⏳ ☐ ○○○○○ ☐

✓ Additional Tasks

1. _____

⏳ ☐ ○○○○○ ☐

2. _____

⏳ ☐ ○○○○○ ☐

Daily Plan
6am
7am
8am
9am
10am
11am
12pm
1pm
2pm
3pm
4pm
5pm
6pm
7pm
8pm

 Strategy Toolbox

- Task Inventory
- Priority Matrix
- 4th Dimension Planning
- Self-Reward
- Chunking
- Flow Sessions
- Temptation Bundling
- _____
- _____

Mood Monitor

Rate Your Day

 **SUNDAY** ___/___/___

★ Priority Tasks

1. _____

⧗ ☐ ⭕⭕⭕⭕⭕ ☐

2. _____

⧗ ☐ ⭕⭕⭕⭕⭕ ☐

3. _____

⧗ ☐ ⭕⭕⭕⭕⭕ ☐

✓ Additional Tasks

1. _____

⧗ ☐ ⭕⭕⭕⭕⭕ ☐

2. _____

⧗ ☐ ⭕⭕⭕⭕⭕ ☐

⚒ Strategy Toolbox

- Task Inventory
- Priority Matrix
- 4th Dimension Planning
- Self-Reward
- Chunking
- Flow Sessions
- Temptation Bundling
- _____
- _____

Daily Plan
6am
7am
8am
9am
10am
11am
12pm
1pm
2pm
3pm
4pm
5pm
6pm
7pm
8pm

Mood Monitor

Rate Your Day

Executive Skills Inventory
End of the Quarter

	Want to Learn	Learning	Mastering
Planning I can break down big projects into manageable steps and estimate how long each step will take me.	☐	☐	☐
Time Management I can get everything done before it causes me problems, and know how to strategize which tasks to do first to stay on top of everything.	☐	☐	☐
Concentration I can sustain focus for longer periods of time, even on tasks I don't "like". My mind, hand, body, and eyes can be on the task in front of me for 20-60 minutes at a time.	☐	☐	☐
Self-control I can notice urges that do things that don't align with my goals and values, and I can stop myself from doing them before they happen, even when this means doing something I don't like doing.	☐	☐	☐
Memory I can remember instructions, lists, and facts both in the short-term and for longer-term needs. When I need this information to help me complete a task or meet a goal, I can recall it easily and accurately.	☐	☐	☐
Flexibility I understand things don't always go as planned, and when the unexpected happens I can make in-the-moment decisions that I feel proud of now and later. Changes don't stress me out because I know they are a natural part of life.	☐	☐	☐
Attention I can choose what my brain pays attention to, even if it's something that doesn't feel "fun". My brain can filter out sounds, sights, and thoughts I don't need to help me focus.	☐	☐	☐
Organization I can organize my belongings and thoughts in ways that make sense to myself and others. I use organization as a tool to help me complete tasks more easily.	☐	☐	☐
Task Initiation I can see a project as a series of small tasks, and I can start the first step independently and quickly, even when I don't feel like it.	☐	☐	☐
Perseverance I can "push through" a task I don't want to do. This can be when it feels boring, long, or hard. Even though I'd like to quit, I keep going.	☐	☐	☐

Executive Skills Inventory

Self-Reflection

In which EF skills did you see the most growth?

_____

_____

_____

_____

Which skills are still most challenging?

_____

_____

_____

_____

Action Steps: *Which of these options do you think would be useful for having even more growth with EF skills? Check all that apply.*

☐ **The planner was helpful. I'd like to keep using a DOING planner.**

☐ **I don't really understand some of the lessons and would like more information about the following:**

☐ **I felt like I gained a lot of good skills and can manage my tasks independently.**

☐ **I feel like I need a partner to help hold me accountable for using my EF strategies and would like to schedule daily or weekly check-ins with a peer or adult.**

A Final Note

Most of us have not magically mastered our minds and feelings in the course of a school quarter. If you have, congratulations! I certainly have not. Even though I practice these skills regularly and find them useful and effective, I am still learning and growing. It's a life-long goal. I consider myself a very productive person, but there are projects I dread and feel an urge to avoid. When this happens, I use strategies to help myself initiate the task and persevere through it. For example, I hate folding laundry, but I let myself watch Netflix on my phone while I fold (temptation bundling), and can almost look forward to it. (Almost.)

Anyway, I hope sharing these strategies felt helpful as you continue your journey to become the master of your own mind and feelings. May you harness all your strengths to help you meet your goals effectively. Keep practicing! I'm almost forty, and I will do the same!

If you have a story to tell or advice to share about your productivity journey, I'd love to hear it! Send me an email at info@MontessoriMindsConsulting.com.

Good luck on your action research (called "life") moving forward. We are all scientists figuring things out as we go. You are your own best teacher.

Sincerely,

Jess

Jess Davis, MEd (Elementary I-II) lives in Bloomington, Indiana and is a parent of three sons. She was a Montessori student and parent, and taught lower elementary for over a decade before moving into administration as Assistant Head of School at a nonprofit Montessori school serving 234 children ages 3-12. She is also the Owner and Lead Consultant of Montessori Minds Consulting, which helps empower students, educators, and schools to meet their goals and fulfill their visions.

Resources

Di Stefano, Giada and Gino, Francesca and Pisano, Gary and Staats, Bradley R., Learning by Thinking: How Reflection Can Spur Progress Along the Learning Curve (February 6, 2023). Harvard Business School NOM Unit Working Paper No. 14-093, Kenan Institute of Private Enterprise Research Paper No. 2414478, Available at SSRN: https://ssrn.com/abstract=2414478 or http://dx.doi.org/10.2139/ssrn.2414478

How to Stay Focused: 10 Tips to Improve Your Focus and Concentration. (2019, October 16). Healthline. https://www.healthline.com/health/mental-health/how-to-stay-focused#avoid-multitasking

Meier, J. D. (2010). Getting results the Agile way : a personal results system for work and life. Innovation Playhouse.

Reflecting on Work Improves Job Performance. (2014, May 5). Harvard Business School. https://www.library.hbs.edu/working-knowledge/reflecting-on-work-improves-job-performance

Schrager, S., & Sadowski, E. (2016). Getting More Done: Strategies to Increase Scholarly Productivity. Journal of Graduate Medical Education, 8(1), 10. https://doi.org/10.4300/JGME-D-15-00165.1

The Myth of Multitasking | Psychology Today. (n.d.). Www.psychologytoday.com. https://www.psychologytoday.com/us/blog/creativity-without-borders/201405/the-myth-of-multitasking

Printed in the United States
by Baker & Taylor Publisher Services